WHAT WOULD JESUS BUY?

FABULOUS PRAYERS IN THE FACE OF

THE SHOPOCALYPSE

REVEREND BILLY

WHAT WOULD JESUS BUY?

FABULOUS PRAYERS IN THE FACE OF
THE SHOPOCALYPSE

PublicAffairs

New York

For information, address PublicAffairs, 250 West 57th Street,
Suite 1321, New York, NY 10107. PublicAffairs books are available at
special discounts for bulk purchases in the U.S. by corporations, institutions,
and other organizations. For more information, please contact the Special Markets
Department at the Perseus Books Group, 11 Cambridge Center,
Cambridge, MA 02142, call (617) 252–5298, or email
special.markets@perseusbooks.com.

Book design by Mark McGarry
Set in Scala with Rosewood display

Library of Congress Cataloging-in-Publication Data
Talen, William.
What would Jesus buy? : fabulous prayers in the face
of the shopocalypse / Reverend Billy. —1st ed.
p. cm.
ISBN-13: 978-1-58648-447-7 (hardcover : alk. paper)
ISBN-10: 1-58648-447-8 (hardcover : alk. paper)
1. Shopping—Humor. 2. Religion—Humor. I. Title.
PN6231.S5467T35 2006
818'.60208—dc22
2006027762

—

FIRST EDITION
10 9 8 7 6 5 4 3 2 1

This book is dedicated to the singers and musicians in the

Stop Shopping Gospel Choir, without whom

Savitri and I would not survive

The Shopocalypse.

CONTENTS

WHAT IS THE SHO·PO·CA·LYPSE?

THE FABULOUS WORSHIP BEGINS.
SISTER MISHAN CLEANSES THE LENS.

AS THE DEVIL'S LOGOS force us up onto the Interstates, we'll be damned if we can tell—hey, am I just driving home from work again or is this the FINAL MOMENT OF HUMAN HISTORY? It's so hard to know, because the Shopocalypse is coming through the dash in the form of a sexual whisper, and it says *"This is Convenience."*

We believe this—as the ocean rises and shoots through our windows. And we keep believing it, as our families are clicked-and-dragged across miles of pavement into Free Speechless big boxes. Do I have a witness? As the Smart Monks from here at the Slow Down Your Consumption School of Divinity have said, "Stop! Stop shopping! Stop!"

Now children, we are all Shopping Sinners. Each of us is walking around in a swirl of gas and oil, plastics and foil. We should all hit our knees and weep and confess together. We are not evil people, but somehow we have allowed the Lords of Consumption to organize us into these mobs that buy and dispose, cry and reload. Yes, the Rapture of the Final Consumption, the Shopture, is underway.

The fundamentalist consumers are lifted way up into the air, into the Supermall of Eternal Convenience, where there are thousands of big boxes and chain stores above the clouds, and where even breathing is on credit. Stadium-sized crowds of the Saved, entire qualifying hordes, are "shoptured up" into a staggering array of discount opportunities. Those of us down here below have been left to die because we have an uneasy feeling about all the Chosen People talk coming out of Davos and Bentonville. Yes, we walked away from the BLOW-OUT CLEARANCE SALE.

As we witness more hapless consumers vortexing straight up into the Supermall of Eternal Convenience, their second America, we must grab their ankles and pull them down, screaming, from their advertopia. They will think we're Devils, of course. They may slap at us as we cling to their shoes and as the sales pass through to the sky. But be gracious. Simply say, "Hello, we are from the Church of Disturb the Customers. Your shopping is ending the world."

What if we could all hear each other, and we could town-cry that WE HAVE AN EMERGENCY. A real community knows how to call out a general, spontaneous warning. In the Church of Stop Shopping, we have seen the word Shopocalypse create a true community the second we shouted it in the Armageddon of a ten-acre Wal-Mart parking lot. We've seen lumbering Teamsters and Hispanic grandmothers and teenage Peace bloggers suddenly hold hands and shout that word in perfect unison. All together now. SHOPOCALYPSE! LET'S STOP IT!

THE SPRING SERVICE

The Love-a-lujah! Revival

OR

Stop Shopping, Start Loving

⁓ ⁓

I love you without knowing how, or when, or from where. . . .
I love you because I know no other way.

PABLO NERUDA

THE REVEREND AND OUR DIRECTOR, SAVITRI D,
PRACTICING LOVE-A-LUJAH!

GREETINGS CHILDREN. Let's talk about Love. One of the Archangels in the Church of Stop Shopping, Emma Goldman, says Love is very powerful. How powerful?

Love, the strongest and deepest element in all life,
the harbinger of hope, of joy, of ecstasy; love, the defier of all laws,
of all conventions; love, the freest, the most powerful
moulder of human destiny . . .
EMMA GOLDMAN

Love-a-lujah!

A couple decades ago, on the evening news, a small group of very earnest scientists, wearing their white lab coats and sweating heavily in front of the cameras, announced that they had discovered "Love." The press conference was intriguing. The lead researchers were three unheard-of professors, who glowed with their triumph. "Yes, we have found the Source! The human species has never had a map to that great bright city called Love."

Well, those are my words.

These happy men of science had isolated the pheromones that we emit from the bridge of our nose. Then, sensing the emissions of others, we may turn toward a certain person in a crowd and find ourselves utterly smitten. Suddenly we start doing grand, stupid things, sometimes for five minutes but sometimes for the rest of our lives . . . Does anyone here recognize what I'm saying? Do I have a witness?

Looking back on it, I think it's strange that these researchers would believe that they had trapped and taken specimens of Love itself. It also feels wildly weird that they would think that we, the people, would be thrilled to have "solved the problem" of Love. The unknowability of Love drives 92 percent of all the songs that we sing (perhaps more, the figures are not in yet!) Our bafflement and aching and comic suicides echo inside a blinding tunnel of Love.

We in the Church of Stop Shopping are dedicated to this consternation. This is among the most serious jobs we have in our human project. We are Fools For Love. And is this bad? Did the scientists really believe that we would have it another way? Did they believe that Lovers everywhere would be better at making Love after seeing the mystery chemically broken down on a chalkboard? Would Love songs now begin to make references to the chemical manufacturing facility that heats the holy steam between our eyes?

Did the Chris Columbuses of Love sell their research to L'Oréal or Revlon? And if not, why not? Pick a company (most of them, it seems) whose principle image is of young, handsome people who are looking out from the product packaging. As they do, trying to catch our consumer's eye, these actors have expressions on their faces somewhere between orgasmic and, let's say it, rapturous. Presumably the corporations would invest heavily in the Viagra of the Big Crush. Wouldn't the marketing departments just love to manipulate the first moment of Love? The gleam in the eye across the room goes NUCLEAR!

My guess is that our excited scientists did peddle a "Love Potion #9" to the beauticians and pharmaceuticals. My second guess is that THE CORPORATE LOVE RESEARCH STARTED LONG AGO. Major emotions are markets, and corporations are nothing if not desperate for Love. In fact, they date us, don't they? Shall we make Confession? When we are whispering intimately, sitting on the fire escape, holding hands, the Corporation is with us. As we turn to face one another, both of us wondering if we will make love, the Corporation is wondering, too. Yes, the Corporation is always there to help in any way that it can. We begin our caresses and the Corporation races toward our bed. It is sighing, moaning, and whispering intimately. It offers us the digital music that we need, the humidity control, and advice on the bedroom paint scheme.

Thank the Fabulous Unknown that when we finally begin to gasp in sweet dirty epithets, we are no longer rational. Marketers lose our trail as we scream and scream.

But children, there *is* something in this hapless story that does leave us with a bit of faith, hope, and charity.

We should be encouraged that these three science guys were greeted by a great thud of silence from the world of lovers . . . from those of us who do the actual loving out here. Forget the corporations—We, The Lovers—we just turned away. We declined to dance with these heavy-breathing whitecoats.

Clearly, we demand mystery. We require an absence of explanation for our Love. We cannot do without our bafflement, aching, and foolish tunnels of Love. Without the mystery, how would Marvin Gaye have found the motivation for his long high howls? In fact, every culture has its favored love-howlers. You see—Love may be mysterious, but it is not nothing. We know how real it is when Marvin sings and a million of us sing back. It is the always-present Fabulous Unknown.

Personally, instead of accepting outside counsel, I prefer to buy flowers, run five blocks, and get a door slammed in my face. Now, *this is living!* If I knew it all and controlled it all, how would I take another step in life and be interested? I am a human being. I am a Man. Spelled M—A—N. In fact, I'm a Preacher Man, spelled P—R—E—, well. . . . Listen, children.

One of my job descriptions is to set out in the pursuit of Love without a map, to have a press conference of a different kind. The great writer Kenneth Patchen had a phrase, "the amorous orator on the village green." I have always thought that a preacher should talk about Love. Yes, if God is Love then a preacher ought to love Love . . .

And if God were the mayor of a bright city of Love, then the citizens of that town would smile and pursue one another according to laws that cannot be written on a chalkboard or sold for money.

Feel like you know the place? Love-a-lujah!

And now, The Reading of the Word, one of the first great love songs:

> *I am come into my garden, my sister, my spouse: I have*
> *gathered my myrrh with my spice; I have eaten my honey-*
> *comb with my honey; I have drunk my wine with my milk:*
> *eat, O Friends; drink, yea, drink abundantly, O beloved.*
>
> THE SONG OF SOLOMON, CHAPTER 5:1

Children, what were you thinking when you heard these words? Yes, me too.

The congregation will please rise. It is time to sing a hymn.

The following could be sung by the Song of Solomon author from those millennia ago, if she time-beamed herself

into a seedy cabaret. Please sing this hymn in a sexy chan-
teusey sigh, next to a late-night piano with darkness and cigarette smoke. Or not. Go goth punk death metal. . . .

Are You My Lover? Or Are You My Logo?

Across a darkened room
I'm not talking, but I interrupt.
You're so . . . slow motion.
You try to sip but not kiss the cup.

You find a way to ask me.
You've got to know, you've got to savor.
The conversation turns and . . .
Well do I—don't I—have a Lover?

Well, do I have a Lover?
What a question in a dump like this,
But do you have a Logo?
My remote's on the screen of a big screen kiss.

What company are you with?
Oh this? . . . it's my new tattoo.
I'm feeling lots of Logo here,
It's crawling up my leg like you.

I'm listening to your Logo.
You whisper in my ear "now dance."

A thousand songs in storage
Reach through my wire like a thin white lance.

You tell me now "get bolder."
You'll have new graphics every week.
And if I say I'm lonely,
Your company tattoo is on my cheek.

I find a way to ask you.
I've got to savor, I got to know.
The conversation turns and . . .
Are you my Lover? Or are you my Logo?

The congregation will please be seated.

Children, welcome all to the Church of Stop Shopping Start Loving. What a pleasure it is to see you beautiful lovers in the pews today. Our message this morning concerns the thorny issue of Love.

Now Saint Emma tells us that Love overrules Laws. I would like to add that gay marriage is the power and the glory and is the key to reversing global climate change brought on by trapped greenhouse gasses. Furthermore, lesbian marriage is the life everlasting and will save the Spotted Owl. Allow me a moment or two and I will explain how this can be.

As society slowly rises from a time that historians will

call the Dark Ages With Irony, a time when whole continents of people dropped their jaws and frowned for days, a time where elephantized humans called celebrities advanced toward ordinary people like the heads on Easter Island secreted through wires and emerging on flickering glass walls. We are, despite all, now pulling ourselves up by our own sexual rainbow, letting the gasps and giggles of personal growth fall where they may, as we dress up and go down to City Hall, with the phallic up-thrust columns of its neo-Roman façade, with its lawyers in suits, clearing their throats. See you at the Court House! I'll see you there and we can publicly acknowledge what we've always done and always will do.

But Gay marriage must be more than just an Issue, children. Issues Schmissues. There is only one fact and that is the fact of Love. The same-sex betrotheds are being patient with our "Issue" because that is the stuck state of our language. That is how our description of this woman–woman man–man holy act goes out across the world, at present. We are working within the limits of language, which creates a label to accommodate our fear of same-sex Love that is long-lived, fiercely defended, and just plain sad.

Now help me. You see, sexual fear always moved words around and created JUDGEMENT LABELS, but we live in a time when lies-in-labeling is in the virulent wind of the Shopocalypse. We must not underappreciate the weird copyright on desire that commercial Puritanism claims. The Puritanized Evil of the babbling of products, of, in a word, *adver-tising*, falsely refracts the act of Love into a thousand little dances, each dance with a product waiting coyly at the end of the night. It's very easy to spin off Gay marriage like a marketing niche. Soon everyone forgets that it was always Love. It becomes more Gay marriage, the product, and less Love, the actual life. And as it becomes an Issue, a Label, a Type, it becomes more an abstract idea of evil, and less the happy commitment that anyone who feels love in any form would always wish on others.

And sex? Would someone who has had happy sex of any kind naturally wish it for others? Sex in any form? No, sexual fear—jealousy, and especially on the massive tribal level—was always a human nightmare. But in the age of Consumption we have particular frustrations that colorize the green jealousy. We are surrounded by images of Love, unlike any other time in history. We are left in the paralyzed masturbatory moment of SHOPPING, halfway to that paradise but never quite there. Kate Moss' mouth is open, and it's a hundred feet across, but WHY? Marketed sex, in our present epoch, must interrupt us—even as we chase it with our dollars and pounds. SEX SELLS, BUT NOT IF IT ACTUALLY TAKES PLACE. Do I have a witness?

Children—in today's Burning Hell of marketing—the memory of Love splatters into 500 channels and a million pixels and it can be forgotten even by good people. Sex is so over-produced and under-actualized, we can't find it any-more. So we have this job: putting the thousand fake sex dances of commodified sin back together again, and letting them cohere into one major velvet maelstrom. Put our public Love back together again.

And that *is* what our sermon is about today, congrega-tion. Let's make a plan, shall we? Turn now to Matthew chap-ter 6 verse 4, "And Jesus saith, Verily verily I say unto you, LOVE IS NOT A NEW AGE CON JOB." It is distinct. It is real. Love is the power and the glory. It is so not sentimental. It is in fact a question of life and death, a key to our survival here in the face of The Shopocalypse.

Love is the force in life that knows that life will survive if life is loved.

Just one minute. Believers and sinners. Can you hear me? I think that somebody needs to hear this ONE MORE TIME . . .

Love is the force in life that knows that life will survive if life is loved.

If you interrupt Love because you stand beneath your neo-Roman up-thrust phallic column in your suit, clear your throat and pronounce that a certain kind of Love is inciting Issues, Legal Precedents, Bad for Jobs, Bad for Families—OH IMPROPER!!—Love, in our species, in our society, picks up on this right away. Love knows. Love won't give Life its for-ward motion if you allow some of it and not all of it. Do I have a witness? Love is the Fabulous Unknown. Love is the Impresario that directs Shocking Evolution. Love *knows*. Love is, you see, residing in both the mind and the heart, as well as behind the bridge of the nose and below the belt. Love *knows*.

Let's make a deal. Shake on it. Love will survive. Amen? That means we can't interfere. Let it go and it will persevere right through whatever fearful fundamentalist culture has been sold as normal. The life with enough Love in it will find a way to live on. Oh! There's that round again—Love in Life knows Life lives on—and this is the strong survival Love that same-sex lovers have given us over the years, as they overcome the hatred and fear.

You see, Life on this Earth isn't separate from any social justice struggle. It's too late in the game to separate these things. Issues will not be isolated from each other when the Earth is extinguished. When you look into the eyes of the person standing next to you and that person is having trouble breathing and you realize that this is the last breath you yourself will be taking because the world has, in fact, JUST ENDED, then all these issues are one. In that last gasp all the progressive Issues are simply Love, and all the advertisements are simply Love mocked to death.

May the Fabulous Unknown that passeth all understanding and doesn't look back, keep us and guide us now and forever.

Amen and Changelujah!

Oh God That Is Not A Product—

Let Love floor us with its mutating foolishness. May we encourage a great exodus of lovers from the beige partitions and the big boxes, from the academies of fear and utopias of falsified desire. Love is the basis of trust, of community, and all the gift economies. . . . May we minister to the drifting consumer infidels stranded in the dumb fluorescence of chain stores and strip malls. And let us Love the consumers. Love even the managers and the rent-a-cops and CEOs and the shareholders. This we ask with no corporate sponsorship, but only the unknowability of Love and a deep creative sense of unquenchable horniness.

God help us.

As you gather your coats to leave, each of you sinners, as a parting gesture, now hug the person sitting next to you. Go ahead. The Stop Shopping Gospel Choir are stranger-hugging practitioners. Am I right, singers? We all ask you to really relax into this hug of the stranger next to you. Yes, feel the heart beating inside that neighbor of yours, and look at that lovely face, look into those big wet eyes.

Those of you in the book-reading congregation, promise your pastor that you will do the same—give a long, nearly inappropri-

ate hug to the next person you encounter in the course of your day. If that next person preempts your hug by, say, sitting in a car, or, worse yet, being a Pope, then do the next most inappropriate thing. If the person is in a car, hug the hood and kiss their window. If they roll the window down, say, "Can I walk you home? That's so cool. Walking home is global cooling."

If the next person you meet IS the Pope, well wow, then hugging is prohibited within a holy mile, but if the pontiff passes by at least give a good shout—I LOVE YOU JOE—YOU GOTTA NICE DRESS!

START YOUR OWN CHURCH—

RETAIL INTERVENTIONS

WAITING FOR THE ACTION MANAGER'S SIGNAL IN A
BOSTON STARBUCKS. THE CASH REGISTER,
SOON TO BE EXORCISED, IS TO MY LEFT.

THE FIRST JOB of a church is to save souls. And pulling out of the advertising/debt/waste cycle of Consumerism is our idea of deliverance. Much of our soul-saving mission work consists of dramatic rituals and plays inside retail environments. Our missionaries are sometimes disguised as consumers—"invisible" to management's eye. At other times our Nonviolent Disobedient Performances inside the retail environment, the chaos and broad strokes— the Inappropriate Behavior! Amen!—carries our message best. The interventions that follow, developed over the last ten years, are some of our favorites.

As your new church prepares to Stop the Shopping of the citizenry, as you become a Sacred Spy of the Shopocalypse, it is worth asking yourself a few questions.

Who's your Devil? Whether it's a big box or chain store, or a nuke plant on a fault line: This is your "charged stage." The consumers are the souls that must be saved. (But never forget: WE ARE ALL SINNERS.) When the consumers come into view, browsing or walking up the street, they will see your church performing inside, or Oddly near, the Devil's logo. We must not be naïve about how powerful the multinationals are in the ordinary matter of BUY THIS. The consumers, upon seeing the imagery of the product or corporation, often immediately have memories, fantasies, anticipations. This is Product Sex, and it is sinning of a very well-defended kind. It is our job to know what the existing props (the logo, celebrity spokesperson, corporate history, recent news items) are doing to the openness of those witnesses. What are they thinking? Could they be open to asking a new question or two about the product before them?

BIG BOXES AND BOUTIQUES

Our local chapter of the Church of Stop Shopping performs in any public setting where we can sing and preach—piers and docks, church rooftops, parks and boulevards. But there will also be "contested" space: the privatized spaces that wish to appear to be public space, but curb our Freedom of Speech. There are two types, the big box and the chain store. These two have their contrasting seductions: the forces behind the fluorescing behemoth big box hope that the stores will glow and call to you with the promise of infinite products; while the chain stores, built to a more human scale, often try to blend in with the neighborhood, sometimes even imitating the local independent shops that they killed.

Retail Interventions in either of these environments can be intimate. We can whisper facts about labor slavery, the history of the company, the CEO's stock options. But when a symbolic pageantry or public drama is staged for visual effect, then the two stages are very different. Big Box stores throw everything into the middle distance *quickly.* Your observers will generally be in cars or behind carts. In the "boutiques," our church activists can sometimes withdraw to the sidewalk or street outside and continue to perform, with the curious customers following us out.

Victoria's Secret and Starbucks are boutiques. Both have managed to depoliticize the public's responses, and remain separate from the phrase "chain store." Victoria's Secret is still not associated in the public mind with clear-cutting virgin forests. Their million catalogs a day are mostly made of virgin timber. Starbucks still insists it has nothing to do with employing seven-year-olds. Starbucks routinely lies about the condition of its coffee worker families. Both companies have more exposure from their famous ads than from the damning research that watchdog groups post on websites. So with these smaller venues, direct education becomes more important. Whatever shocking bit of theater catches our audience's interest, we still must prove our case in a more traditional way with clear and clean information sheets.

This is where a long retreat from a supermall can be an advantage. Once you give a shopper a sheet, security cannot intercede—they don't pull the paper from the customer's hands. So if we are escorted to the door and start walking across the parking lot, we might hand out information to a hundred people walking in from their cars. (It is fascinating to have later email conversations with people you encounter in the malls, and it helps spread the Word. Always make it easy for the shoppers to contact you.)

Where to Begin

Case the joint thoroughly. In the days before your Action, as you walk through the target store, slow yourself down and . . . slow the products down, too. See through them. Watch how the branding works. A Nike store is covered with the flying sweating limbs of the famous. A McDonald's is so bright the air has an ice-like quality, but smells like fries. A Starbucks is dedicated to uniformity but with items that suggest originality, such as mismatching beatnik-like furniture.

These Evil nonplaces each dare us to answer with the perfect violation, the introduction of an internal opposition that explodes the picture. We hope that you find an Action wonderfully suited to cave in the propaganda of your Devil store. We hope these sketches of Actions free your own imagination in these imagination-killing settings.

From the Mouths of Babes to the Blog of the Church

At many Art Attacks there are three types of witnesses: the people, the press, and the police. The latter two are media—they send the message out by way of *their* theater and so they are important. And you should know who will be there and what to do if a badge or microphones are suddenly thrust in your face.

But the first witness is the people. They are often there shopping and we are hoping to interrupt them in an entertaining way. We want to help them create a folk story from their experience. It is always a pleasure to overhear one of them weeks after an Action, "I saw this terrible marriage spat. It was in the middle of the mall. The wife was describing a sweatshop factory and the husband was on his knees. He was absolutely wretched. He was begging her not to leave him because he bought a Tickle-Me-Elmo that was made in Sri Lanka or somewhere. I mean, he was groveling . . . it was incredible!" Don't be fooled into thinking that this is just light comedy. This is the heart of the matter. This is NEW. To us this is the birthing of new anti-Shopocalyptic language.

A key to change is found in the talk of interrupted shoppers. Communicate. Try to hear what is being said on the grapevine, on blogs, find out what others are doing with their impressions. Post it all on your website, send it all to ours! Revbilly.com! OH PRAISE! WHEN THE SHOPPING STOPS!

Role Players

Every Art Attack should have an Action Manager (AM). Most of the thirteen Actions described below have steps in them and the manager can signal when to stand up and sing, to go to the climax of the piece, or to suddenly go mute if the police happen by. Oftentimes the AM stands near the front door or window, to see both into the store and out into the surrounding cityscape.

It helps to also have a Physical Educator. This is someone who can really lead warm-ups in the church basement, a church members' yard, or a public park. Breaking through the strict choreography of products and retail environments takes body-and-soul readiness. When you Disturb The Customers, you are doing hard work. Usually we're basking in the pleasurable release of it for hours afterward, but we're sore the next morning. Breathing and stretching beforehand helps.

Arrange for your Fair Witness. You'll want to get a later critique from someone not involved in the Action itself, someone who sits on the very edge of the whole play and can see all the elements. This person is not holding a spy cam or watching for police. His or her only job is to see it all.

And always be polite to the workers and customers. Most of these Actions are comedies with a social conscience. But comedy is very close to anger, and excites all kinds of stuff in onlookers . . . know that border. Don't be angry at anyone who is angry with you. They may be dealing with the breaking apart of Living Through Products, a fundamentalist faith, oppressive and hard to leave behind.

Stay soft, cunning, loving.

DIRECT ACTION WORKBOOK

— ❧ —

13 RETAIL INTERVENTIONS FOR
YOUR ACTION PLEASURE

— ❧ —

Bump and Grind the Buckheads

Gather a large number of party-prone faithful. Have on hand (printed on two sides so as to save paper) many copies of the Coverco report (which you can get at www.coverco.org.gt/e_index.html) in both English and Spanish. There are lousy things in that report about people who bring non-Fair Trade coffee to market. The study took place in Guatemala, and a lot of Starbucks's victims are kids. (They have to work all day, no school, bad food, no health care. The ratio of people to doctors in the Western Highlands of Guatemala is 85,000-to-1 and Howard Schultz is a billionaire, but I'm preaching.) Instruct everyone to stuff the pages of this report into their trouser legs, stockings, panties, undershirts, and bras.

Enter and fill up a Starbucks with this large group until the ratio of people to floor space is like a hot club on Saturday night. Go with saxophonists, kazoos, guitars, a Trinadadian drum . . . whatever noise and music-makers you have. Add a blaster with Thelonius Monk—or whatever moves your soul.

(Don't use music whose soul was sold to Starbucks!) Press the ON button. Ask the musicians to play. Begin to dance. Everyone bumps and grinds while the shoppers try to sip their $4 non-Fair-Trade lattes. The bumping and grinding gives way to increasingly articulate stripping. The reports fly out of the underclothing like bilingual white doves. Our experience: Some sippers are annoyed, some get up and dance. Anybody who has questions, you can talk and rock at the same time, or leave together and keep discussing. Bump and Grind them Beans!

Your AM is watching from the sensible perspective and will let you know when you should remove yourself to DANCING IN THE STREETS! Amen.

Commercial Free Zone

Gather twenty or more of your worshippers outside, in an advertising-heavy area. In New York?—of course, Times Square. Special roles: a couple loud-mouth preachers or street barkers, a couple angels dressed in white, and one flutist—or a musician that makes us dream.

Make a circle. Stand the faithful shoulder to shoulder, facing outward at the high pressure media-sphere. Give everyone in the circle a big white cardboard panel and ask them to hold each panel up so that the bottom of the rectangle is just above their eyes. The panels are held edge to edge, so that, with the bodies of the faithful, a great circular room is created. On each panel is a giant letter, so that pedestrians and motorists can read the phrase: "COMMERCIAL FREE ZONE."

In the center of the circle, behind everyone's behind, place a number of beautiful plants. On a plush rug set love seats or a relaxing-looking couch. Next to the little forest with the furniture, arrange for your flutist to play "Afternoon of the Faun" by Debussy, or something suitably soothing. Outside the circle, the preachers invite the passersby to "COME IN OUT OF THE ADS! SAVE YOUR ODD AND HOLY SOUL FROM THIS PREDATORY ECONOMY! NO SELLING HERE IN OUR SPECIAL WILDERNESS AREA, CHILDREN! COME AND RELAX! We'll protect you! No ads will reach you! Inside this circle is a special place to have a moment to yourself, admiring the backsides of the Commercially Free, and listening to music's idea of an eternal afternoon. You can come here and STOP YOUR SHOPPING!"

When a stray soul accepts your invitation, the angels accompany her or him delicately through the circle to the paradise within. Trust them to be alone there, but come to their aid if they have a request. Leave a glass of water on the table.

Be gentle with your recovering souls. You can even let them fall asleep. Ask for a thought when they are ready to leave. Thank them for joining you, just as you would if they had been in your home. Thank the musician!

What's That Voice in the Mickey T-Shirts?

Prerecord messages from sweatshop testimonies onto a dozen cheap tape recorders (". . . my salary comes to fourteen cents an hour..."). These remarkable and painful statements from those young people trapped in the globalized economy are available from http://www.nlcnet.org/resources—*the website of the National Labor Committee.*

Now go into a sweatshop company's outlet—a Disney store or Wal-Mart will do fine. Place the tape recorders down in the products, such as under sweatshirts or behind boxes. Press play. (You should have left a little leader of blank tape so that you have time to walk away before the sound starts up.) A few steps from where you planted your Seed of Truth, you can watch the comedy heat up.

Soon sweatshop workers' words are popping out ("I SIT THERE AT THE SEWING MACHINE UNTIL I FALL ASLEEP!") all over the store from beneath the products they manufactured. Security officers confer and start digging for the truth. Sometimes we the Humble Servants pile on the mischief. We have seen a Stop Shopping parishioner become incensed, scolding a Disney guy, "How could you allow these sweatshop workers to enter my delicate Disney experience! This is the High Church of Retail! This is my Holy Moment!"

We should admit that one obvious flaw of this Action is that it pressures the workers present on the retail floor, who are also often underpaid, may have been denied union rights, and probably agree with the feelings we have about sweatshops. If it's any comfort—it's the store managers who usually resemble Keystone Kops as they toss sweatshirts over their heads, desperate to hit the OFF button of the suffering.

Shop Lift!

This is one of the simplest yet most powerful Actions. It helps in this Action if the participants are world diverse. It's quick: You can hit a number of stores in succession, and because, like Bump and Grind, it is Body Theater (our bodies make the drama here), you'll want a big tight crowd in the store.

File into the Devil's chain store. On the signal from the Action Manager, lift store items up high over your heads. All the chairs, ashtrays, napkin dispensers, gum machines, products—everything in the store that isn't nailed down is hovering up there, held aloft. Now your prayer-leader makes a statement about the origins of these objects.

So this Action requires good research. The prayer is a direct-address to the people who made these things. Close your eyes with the store's assets and inventory suspended above you and give the prayer its powerful send-off. We call this a Push Prayer. "We know that you have made these products. We feel your touch on these things that surround us . . ."

If these are Wal-Mart clothes, have a Chinese American member of the church call out in Cantonese or Mandarin to the workers on the other end of the labor loop. What an honest feeling to get this message going in the language of the workers as well as the consumers. Make a request that "somehow the division between consumers and workers be ended, so that we can talk directly to each other. So that we can talk to you.

"There is a silence in this thing I have up here in my hand, a vision is locked in this, a witnessing. We upset the product from its presentation, take it back a step toward you. The journey of these products keeps us apart, the false 'Free Market' keeps us apart, and we are both powerless and we are both poor because we are kept apart. We believe that you hear us in the sweatshops and that we hear you calling from your toxic fields and when the distance in this product is finally crushed that we will touch."

Carefully put the items down—so as not to damage them—and exit the store. This can be solemn. Or it can be joyous!

First Amendment Mob

This one can be wonderful with ten people, and wonderful with 300 people. It's eerily the same, regardless of how many of you recite it. The important thing is—when a public place has been the setting for an arrest, say, in which the police forgot about the Bill of Rights, then we go to that corporate lobby, or park, or river shore line, and begin to recite together the single sentence that is the First Amendment:

> Congress shall make no law respecting an establishment of religion, or prohibiting the free exercise thereof; or abridging the freedom of speech, or of the press; or the right of the people peaceably to assemble; and to petition the government for redress of grievances.

Now this also works well talking into cell phones. Some of our Odd Believers feel safer with that cover. You can pretend that you're talking to a niece that is trying to memorize it for a school class. This gives you the pretext for repeating it over and over again. If you were talking on the cell to your niece, you might say, "Alright, Siena, let's go through it one more time, ready? Congress shall make no law . . . " We've also had folks who were talking to friends on cell phones and the people on the other end were helping with the recitation by reading the First Amendment aloud.

But many Holy Mobbers just memorize the beautiful

words, with both hands free to gesture. Some feel that they want to walk and declaim, while others stand there reading the amendment from a piece of paper. There are no mistakes. The sensation of repeating these five freedoms is dependably uplifting—emotionally meaningful to both the recitator and the listener—but this power is hard to explain. We have staged this Action in places that are deeply contested, where governments and corporations are struggling for supremacy over individuals and community. But police have never been able to arrest us, halting in midcuffing, then looking around bewildered by their sudden lack of power as the Amendment echoes around us.

At Ground Zero, we gathered to recite these freedoms for forty straight Tuesdays running up to the 2004 Republican National Convention held in New York. The first chance the public had to walk down into the massive construction site was offered by the reconstruction of the World Trade Center train station. So every Tuesday, we would walk with the Wall Streeters, most of them with more-or-less the same jobs as those who had perished. We walked alongside them whispering, striding like commuters, or we walked against the tide, or we stood on prominent spots and shouted. Over the course of the forty Tuesdays, the flouting of the First Amendment in the outside world became more glaring. The police, who at first thought we were insulting their lost friends, got used to us, got to know our first names, and finally some of them, to our surprise, recited alongside us, "Congress shall make no law . . . "

The California Guided Meditation

This Action is well-served with twelve to fifteen participants and one meditation leader. It's ruined if we burst out laughing, but does get funnier the longer it lasts! In Disney stores we do this Action holding hands in a circle around the most prominent stand-alone display, where many famous neurotic cartoon characters look out from the shelves. The leader, walking on the outside of this circle, talks in the high monotone of a yoga instructor or hypnotist. "And now you will close your eyes and give your mind permission, let your mind know, that what you will be seeing over this next period of time, the visions that you will imagine, will come from my instructions and my instructions only."

The leader pauses, then continues, "Now, holding hands in this sacred circle, look deeply into the eyes of the product before you, whether it be Goofy or Pluto or Donald Duck . . . that's right, look deeply into those fierce eyes. That's right. Return the product's stare, bond with it."

The sequence of the guided visualizing may go like this:

1. Look into the eyes of the product.
2. Close your eyes now and let your earliest memory come into your mind. Take your time. Let it come.
3. Very good. You are in a backyard now in a sandbox with

your brothers and sisters. Or you are looking up at your mother from a tricycle. Very good. Now. Introduce the product with which you have bonded, insert that Disney product—that famous bug or fuzzy animal or princess— directly into that early scene. This might not be easy. If you need to open your eyes again so that you can take the Disney character back into your old memory, go ahead. Don't rush it.

4. Alright? Very good, now you have introduced into your earliest memory a new character, some Mickey Mouse or Goofy or Pluto or Donald is right there in the sandbox with you, OK. Everyone got their character in there, in that scene? Very good. But now you have to try to play with it, and it's like a stranger has walked into your world, a monstrous nightmare of a stranger with big crazy eyes and a neurotic screaming voice. You begin to become afraid of it. It's too big. It wants too much. It wants all the attention. Its arms are always reaching, and its eyes bulging. And it suddenly dawns on you that: THIS IS OUTRAGEOUS! Why is your long-ago memory becoming a Disney production anyway? Now I want you to let yourself feel betrayal and anger. Give yourself permission to be hurt . . .

5. Open your eyes and shout into the eyes of that Goofy or Pluto or Donald: "I reject you! I throw you out! MY LIFE IS

NOT A DISNEY PRODUCTION! I am free of your entertainment, your insinuation into my intimate memories . . .

6. Break from holding hands, and everyone run from the store. Run out onto the sidewalk, into the street. (Careful!) You're shouting "I am free of Disney! My life is not a Disney Production! I am free! I am free!"

Lost and Found

This can be one person, or can be several. Simply, you pretend to lose something of great importance to you in a crowded room. This can be the waiting area in a train station or an audience waiting for a film to begin. The item should be something laden with memory, something with a backstory. Take your time to think of what your lost treasure could be—perhaps pretend that it is something valuable and old from your own life that you would really hate to lose.

In this example the lost valuable is a great-great-aunt's (the ancestor of a friend of ours) diary, a little leather-bound book. We were entrusted with it—now it's vanished. We are heartbroken and energized and filled with the power of the life in the diary.

As you get on your hands and knees looking in the darkness under chairs, in the seams between sections of couch, behind other people's luggage, you keep describing "The lost world that she wrote about. She was a lesbian! Her name was

Lorraine! Excuse me if I could just look behind here . . . . You see she met her lover in Chicago at a librarian's convention—oh I hope we don't lose this—excuse me can I look behind your leg?—thanks—and the two of them homesteaded in South Dakota for twenty years with seven foster children—have you seen it? A little black book, very old—and then they moved back east when two of the sons went AWOL from the Spanish American War—what a story! We'll just be crushed if we . . . excuse me can I look under here?—and then they started a Peace organization and took in refugees in a Toronto Hotel that they somehow fixed up . . . "

This monologue is an ideal format for re-introducing the bios of the Saints in our church: Mother Jones, Joe Hill, the manong in San Francisco, or Bruce Utah Phillips, King of the Hobos.

The Moral of the Action is: We have lost our histories, but they are within us, under us, in the darkness behind us. Left in the hands of commercial media, the history of change in our society is either erased altogether or is made sentimental and sugary and depoliticized. Let's find our past and say it out loud in public space.

Cell Phone Opera Number One

Works well with between fifteen and twenty-five church members. Enter the store in character as single shoppers. The Church members pretend not to know each other, but everyone has essentially the SAME story. Each of you has been sent by a wife or husband on an errand: to go to this store and buy something for a child's birthday.

One by one you get on your cell phones to object to the choice of gift. The store gradually fills with voices calling home. All of you are disagreeing with that wife or husband who sent you—you refuse to buy the assigned gift. The ferocity of a marriage spat is a very powerful force—phrases like "Look DEAR! Excuse me HONEY!" make rent-a-cops evaporate. If someone does shush you, well, agree and apologize—continue with a harsh whisper through clenched teeth. (Nothing is louder.) Make up some refusenik-style theater: "Do you think Cindy should idolize this Snow White doll? This little wasp waist, c'mon! Oh! Oh! I see—so women's rights never happened is that it? Excuse me Ralph—why am I here? Why am I buying this LITTLE PLASTIC SLUT? ARE YOU TRYING TO ASK ME TO LOSE WEIGHT?"

It is most effective to let the volume of the army of kvetchers stay at a realistic level, then rise very gradually, on maestro-like signals from the AM, so that the social conscience of our innocent browser can be excited several times as he or she walks into the voice-range of one phone call after another. A variation: A wife and a husband suddenly collide with each other shrieking, in front of the Pocahontas pajama sets. "What are you doing here? No YOU told ME to buy this

. . . this sweatshop piece of garbage!" At which point the marriage spat about the gift for Kimmy is free to continue LIVE AND NASTY!

The Action Manager is, as always, on the lookout from the most all-seeing spot, usually near the front door, or by a large window. The signal to leave comes from the AM. We have found that we can usually continue our cell phone conversations as we leave the store—trailing info-sheets on Disney as we exit.

Cell Phone Opera Number Two

This one is meant for Starbucks, in a neighborhood where the Devil's cafes are clustering. How many of the Stop Shopping pious are needed for this Action? Four or five or up to a dozen or more. This is the emergency: Placelessness.

The latte sipper looks up to see a person on a cell phone who is frantically lost, frowning, looking out windows. "But you said Starbucks at Astor Place, and here I am. No I'm not angry. I look forward to meeting you. You looked real wonderful on the Internet, uh . . . and I spent an hour on the subway too . . . so, where are you? Starbucks at Astor Place. Well so am I! Well, there's more than one? Oh. Well, go to the window and look out and wave. Do you see me? I don't see you. Maybe . . . maybe . . . Look, I'll go outside and jump up and down until someone comes by and stops me and maybe that'll be you."

Then a second and a third person on cell phones, just a few feet away, are shouting, "I'm at the Starbucks now! Where are you! What? I'm at the Starbucks. Are you here?" Obviously, it is wonderful to have lots and lots of people lost, asking about other Starbucks, getting directions to other Starbucks, going up to people at their lattes and asking: "Are You My Date?" or "Are You My Date and Are You Changing Your Mind?" or "Have You Seen a Redhead with Bangs and a Tattoo That Says Hildegarde?"

Nice touch: Later, the redhead that has that tattoo shows up asking for the person who just left. It's a "Who's On First" routine.

Note: Placelessness mixes in with identity problems in this Action, because if you don't know where you are, eventually you don't know who you are. Leave an info-sheet with a map to a locally owned Fair Trade coffeeshop.

Trash Worship

Twenty Actioneers dress up like upwardly mobile careerists. Each of you has a briefcase, a gym bag, or a big purse. You enter the Starbucks until the place is full. At least one person is seated at every table, and others are standing by the various counters— every flat surface has a nearby interventionist.

On the AM's signal, begin to lift out of your briefcases the empty Starbucks cups that you previously culled from the trash. Do this without expression, studying each item with interest, placing the cup carefully on the table. Soon the tables are crowded with Starbucks' cups. There is no more room for anything else. You are sitting in this forest of upright trash, every item sporting the Starbucks logo. Then something very dramatic and Odd happens. Gypsy dancers stage a grand entrance through the front door of the Starbucks, accompanied by wild Bulgarian violinists. (Or your variation of same: this could be a fiery flamenco diva, or an elegant Degas-like ballerina, or a step-dancer in clogs.)

The dancers have their skirts in their fists, flashing red petticoats. They throw back their heads keening as they whip their skirts around. Instead of clapping, you methodical yuppies at the tables pick up one cup in each hand and wave them in circles in the air. (You come from a mysterious culture in which applause takes the form of this ritual Starbucks cup gesture.) The performers dance frenetically, encouraging more enthusiastic cup circles. Soon the entire Starbucks is full of two-fisted cup circlings and you keep waving the cups until finally the dancers and musicians leave bowing and yipping.

When your play-within-a-play is over, put the cups away, into the briefcases and purses. Leave quietly. To the observer, the whole thing was a strange dream.

Of course, leave behind information sheets about Starbucks abuses.

Virtually Hip

This is a comedy for the Larry, Curly, and Moe of anticon-sumerism. The Action is adaptable to any of the BOBO (bourgeois bohemian) chain stores that pretend to be arty, a destination for the hapless scene-maker or taste-follower: Anthropologie, Crate and Barrel, Urban Outfitters, Starbucks. Take these Three-Stooges-like, over-the-top characters and improvise from there.

As you wander around the store, Hipster #1 feels like he dodged a bullet: He doesn't have to figure out what might be hip anymore. He's SO RELIEVED that the hip decisions have been made by the mysterious gods of retail. He says "Wow, I'm virtually hip! I wanted to be hip all my life and now I'm IN." Hipster #2? He just keeps saying, "Wow I am SO HIGH—this shit is SO GOOD. I'm SAILING. Oooh . . . I'm sailing over the edge. This stuff goes to my source, right to my source. I got to experience this, MORE of this, cause WOW. I'M VIRTUALLY HIP!" And Hipster #3: "I'm completely taken care of. I don't have to have any political values at all. I'm free of 'having a position' or 'feeling involved' and all that HORSESHIT. Yeah, baby, I will never, oh man, all that GUILT! Gone. I am so postsocial, baby. I mean I'm SO social. I mean, I don't know what I mean—I'm passing out. I'm VIRTUALLY HIP."

So: The first hipster has virtual taste, the second virtual physical sensation, and the third virtual social connection. And they are funny in the tradition of the Three Stooges if their three kinds of know-nothingism are performed like fast hand-to-hand contact: biffing each other, farting, belching, apologizing, walking into walls, failing to shop like a civilized human being. This has tremendous dramatic possibilities! The bourgeois bohemian raised to the level of inspired pratfalling. Videotape this, but also leave behind the research about this company—not funny at all.

The Stockbroker and the Mermaid

This is a clash of two archetypes in the lead roles, but there are hidden mermaids—you'll see—and the AM is looking on, ready to join in. The two principals in the Action sit at the same table under the famous Starbucks mermaid-logo. You two will both be claiming ownership of that logo.

First, the broker: You are confessing your love of Starbucks because of its constant expansion. "I love investing in Starbucks. I love to go to Karachi and find that my investment welcomes me—there she is—the green fish-woman in that beautiful logo, another damn Starbucks!"

The church member across the table (can be any gender, of course) turns to the broker and says, "Excuse me, but why did you Starbucks people air-brush the nipples off the Fish-goddess? Her navel is gone too." He replies paternalistically, "Well, ma'am, back in '96 we went into more conservative demographics like Ohio and Dubai—the old logo was actually quite sexy. Can't have that!" The church member replies, "Oh, why do that predictable phallic thing? Expand schmexpand. Just breathe and float in the mermaid's ocean, feel the soft protection of her lovely womb." He edges away from the nut. But she is getting angry. "Look at her in the logo. She is the oceanic fertility goddess of the sea. She is Pina and Fan and Sheel-a-nagig!"

The stockbroker gets a call on the cell. It's the New York Stock Exchange calling. Starbucks has announced a thousand more coffee shops in Africa and the stockbroker has made $100,000 in the last ten minutes. He leaps up from the chair! "ANOTHER TRIPLE LATTE FOR ME! THE MERMAID'S TAKING THE SUBSAHARA LIKE A PACK OF F–16's!"

This trips something in our church member. A mermaid starts to move within her, to kick, to be born. The woman is undulating. We hear a long beautiful moan from the primeval underwater caves. To the astonishment of our Wall Streeter, this mermaid is swimming to the surface. She is a great fish.

"WHAT AM I? I AM BECOMING! I AM THE MERMAID FROZEN IN THE LOGO. AND I WANT MY NIPPLES BACK!" Then she stands on the chair, and then the table. (Careful!) She addresses the whole Starbucks, "YES, I AM THE STARBUCKS MERMAID AND I AM GETTING MY NIPPLES BACK!"

More women rise from surrounding tables. They swim through the Starbucks, out onto the sidewalk and into the next Starbucks. More mermaids emerge, more mermaids, bare-breasted and undulating their fins, it's the Mermaid Parade let loose in the city. "We are the mermaids who swam out of the Starbucks logo, and we have our power!"

Sponsored Lover

Two leads (Jamie and Lucy) and two supporting parishioners (the shills) are needed. If possible each shill has a couple of supporting shills coming in from across the Starbucks to join the debate. This Action is designed to spread. If it's working, a whole Town Hall meeting develops inside our host chain store, discussing the issue of corporate appropriation of human emotions.

Jamie and Lucy are the two lovers. You two enter the store and sit, staring into each others' eyes. Hold hands in the center of the table. You are transfixed, and just a bit loud. Your shills sit nearby with the AM in sight. The AM sizes up the progress of the play and signals all the shills to turn toward the lovers and openly watch, encouraging voyeuristic interest from throughout the coffee shop.

Jamie: "I love you."
Lucy: "Oh, I love you."
Jamie: "I love you."
Lucy: "Yes darling, I love you so much."

Jamie: "I want to elope, marry, everything."

Lucy: "I want to plunge into a new life."

Jamie: "I love you."

Lucy: "I love you, too."

Jamie gets on one knee beside the table.

Jamie: "Will you marry me?, brought to you by Subway—Eat Fresh!"

Lucy: "Oh sweetheart . . . but . . . What did you say?"

Jamie: "What I've been saying all along. I love you, brought to you by Fig Newtons, The Taste Treat from Nabisco."

Lucy: "I love you. Just say 'I love you.'"

Jamie: "I just love you, Lucy, brought to you by Waste Management Systems, WM, Relax—We'll Clean Up!"

Lucy: "Honey, what IS this?"

Jamie: "This is my undying devotion to you, that's all sweetheart, don't be concerned, sponsored by Zocor. It's Your Future. Be There."

Lucy: "Have you, have you . . . SOLD OUR LOVE?!"

Jamie: "Honey, brought to you by your local Coca-Cola bottler, I love you as much as ever! Believe me! by Polo Deckwear."

Lucy: "Oh my god . . . this is a nightmare . . ."

It unravels from there. This little comedy can branch out in several directions. We would like to hear what you come up with—or see your videotape. It's very important for the shills to come over to the lovers and spread the discussion throughout the Starbucks. Be loud enough. Don't be afraid of entering the zone of Exalted Embarrassment.

"Excuse me. I couldn't help but overhear that you found a corporate sponsor for your marriage proposal. That's a fascinating profit center. Very creative, almost artistic. Who do you talk to for that kind of arrangement . . . do you have an agent?"

A second shill approaches in a state of shocked (and loud) disbelief. "Saying 'I love you' with corporate sponsorship? Are you, are you SERIOUS? I just want to say that this is incredible. Has it come to this? What is this culture coming to? ARE YOU INSANE?"

Another shill marches up. "Look, dude, this is the twenty-first century, so get on board or get out of the way. You're either with us or against us. How do you think people make a living today? I've sold ad space on my grandma's forehead!"

The notion that you can sell intimate emotions to corporations is debated by the shills, while the lovers sit in the center of it all. Maybe you'll be lucky and a Joni Mitchell love song will come over the Starbucks sound system . . .

Once we had a little old man speak up. He was the kind of nondescript fellow who might haunt the back pages of a Carson McCullers southern diner, that person who is always quietly there in the back with his newspaper and careful napkin and fork. I noticed him and I thought we must be annoying him. Suddenly he put his paper down and called out— "Did you read the one about the desperate couple who offered to name their child Wal-Mart Lowest Prices Always Johnson? They were demanding a million dollars. Imagine that—growing up with that name. 'Hello who are you?' 'Oh my name is Wal-Mart Lowest Prices Always Johnson!' I mean, what would you call such a child at home? 'Wally'? Yes that's probably what they had in mind. Drop the advertisement in the middle and just stick with Wally but meanwhile get out of town with that Wal-Mart money. Yes, I'm sure of it, that's what they were thinking, that young couple. Oh well, his name is probably Harold now, something like that. Probably Harold Higby Johnson, after some deceased Uncle Harold Higby or some such. Oh well."

He brought down the house.

THE SUMMER SERVICE

The WHAAAA-lujah! Revival,
The Supernatural Hayride,

OR

Stop Shopping, Start Believing

❧ ❧

I have always been regretting that I was not
as wise as the day I was born.

HENRY DAVID THOREAU

BROTHER DERRICK, LEADING US IN THE ATTACK
ANTHEM, STARBUCKS AND DISNEY, IN THE
WGN STUDIO IN CHICAGO.

CHILDREN! Let's start off today's Supernatural Hayride with a little jazz riff on believing.

"Can-you-BELIEVE-this? You-better-BELIEVE-it! Who-knows-what-to-BELIEVE! I-don't-BELIEVE-it. UnBE-LIEVABLE. You-gotta-BELIEVE. Oh, I-don't-BELIEVE-that. BELIEVE-it-or-not. Who-do-you-BELIEVE? Why-should-I-BELIEVE-you? That-is-unBELIEVABLE. If-you-BELIEVE THAT-then-I've-got-a-bridge-for-you-cheap. Please-BELIEVE-me. Are-you-a-BELIEVER?"

Am I a Believer?

We are beaten up by believing. A lot of us don't think belief is the way to go. That's for God-wackos who kill each other, that's for cults and enslavement to branding—humorless armies of one kind or another. So we retreat into passive irony, style, distancing devices—we play it safe. We atomize our opinions into quips. We depoliticize ourselves. We become cultural commitmentphobes. NO BLAME HERE CHILDREN. This move makes sense. It's a defensive position against violence.

But yes we are believers. We must be. It's never been

more important than this moment, in the face of the Shopocalypse, to recover belief . . .

Let's ask the question: Why is having a muscular belief—a belief felt with passion, a belief that can be traced to a single clear statement—why is such a thing necessary? Because we need to perform this creative opposition. We haven't known how to oppose a culture led by Consumerism and apocalyptic Christianity—the twin fundamentalisms that overwhelm governments, silence creative culture or any noncommercial Life, and make routine the crying out of a world of victims. We haven't known what to do, have we? We have not had a consensus for social change in many years.

No, Gabriel is not blowing the right trumpet. John Paul Jones is forgetting to begin to fight. Maybe we have a healthy fear of ideology. We remember all the -isms and the innocents killed. Or maybe we're just haunted. Our old social movements have now become, before our wide eyes, advertising campaigns. Starbucks has systematically taken every movement from labor to ACT UP and created a coffee flavor. Maybe we're afraid that if we reach for the sword of righteousness it will turn into glimmering pixels in our hand.

And so we hesitate. We are mediated, not immediate. When we hesitate for a few minutes or years, well then the shopping pours in that undefended opening. All the discounted luxury items move toward us. The convenience, the ease, the full stop of complete entertainment. We can consume action for the rest of our lives. We can become consumers of change. We are offered every flavor.

Some right-wing finger-waggers might say that we don't have a prayer. Oh yeah?

Let us pray.

We ask the Impresario of Shocking Evolution and Holy Hilariousness: Give us a law, down at the immoveable center, more fun and more fundamental than the fundamentalisms. We ask that we be spared the convenience of aggressive belief. Help us to leave the smart bombs and the afterlife religions on the shelf. Give us a sign. Grant us our faith. Amen.

Can we have a song from the choir now? Yes, here it is, the theme song for the catastrophe, "The Shopocalypse," a bit of that bad convenience we have been discussing. Let it bounce and let it move you like great gospel should.

The Shopocalypse

Will you survive the fire? The Shopocalypse!
Can you feel the heat in this shopping list?
The neighbors fade into the super mall.
The oceans rise but I—I must buy it all.
Shopocalypse, Shopocalypse . . .
It ain't the Blues, it's Convenience!

Will we drive fast all night to the wilderness?
Will we die of fright when the logos hiss?
Can we go home, break in our own front door?
The TV stops to hear our insides roar.
Shopocalypse, Shopocalypse . . .
It ain't the Blues, it's Convenience!

Will a hard rain we pray confuse the darkest gods?
Did Jesus buy on time to improve his Odds?
The brightest lie—it screams into the happy face.
The bluest sky betrays, betrays the human race.
Shopocalypse, Shopocalypse . . .
It ain't the Blues, it's Convenience!

Amen.

Children, let's build our faith now. Ready to believe? We have here a tongue-twister incantation. Let's state this belief nine times. Can we have some help from the drums? Thank you. A One, and a Two, and a Three . . .

We believe in the God that people who don't believe in God believe in.

We believe in the God that people who don't believe in God believe in.

We believe in the God that people who don't believe in God believe in.

We believe in the God that people who don't believe in God believe in.

We believe in the God that people who don't believe in God believe in.

We believe in the God that people who don't believe in God believe in.

We believe in the God that people who don't believe in God believe in.

We believe in the God that people who don't believe in God believe in.

We believe in the God that people who don't believe in God believe in.

Now we're getting somewhere! WATCH OUT! WE BELIEVE!

We human beings always believe in something, in spite of ourselves. So, what is that thing that EVERYONE believes in? Regardless of the gods or brands or atheisms that we've already signed on for? We're looking for a belief that is more basic than all that. We all believe it. Just—ALL OF US— What is it?

At the moment that we are born, we are all members of the same church. It's the God of WHA? WHAT'S GOING ON? And yes, The Late Archbishop of Love, Dr. Reverend Marvin Gaye, is watching over us . . .

Let me try to describe how we ALL OF US are believers

in this particular WHA! faith. All of us at this very moment, wherever we are—in the building, in the street, out on the roads—each of us has back in the deepest darkest part of our brain a single question. And this old question is repeating over and over back there. It keeps repeating the phrase: WHA! WHAT'S GOING ON?

You see, in our church we don't have to be born again, we just want to conjure the feeling of being born the first time. That's amazing enough for us. I mean, how did we respond when we swam out of the underwater light of mom into the harsh light of the birth room? What was that first WHA?

Thoreau is right. We were wise then. And—despite the noise—we were not afraid. We were fully engaged in living, committed, ready, fierce, beyond happy or sad, IN it . . . not afraid of some distant baby with a different color skin than ours. We were reaching for Life and not for a product, so alive we didn't even have to be hopeful . . . alive alive alive . . . living the question: WHAT IS THIS? and loving the asking . . . WHA WHA WHA???

Today's Sunday School assignment: Go out and find the belief that EVERYONE has. Belief-a-lujah! Go out and stand in the center of a large crowd. Imagine that every one of those folks has a voice talking inside their heads, back in their ancient lizard brain. They hear that question WHA? WHAT'S GOING ON? echo from their original personal Big

Bang—the jolt of being born. When we slid from Mom, we had to wonder, we had to cry out that unanswerable question: WHA? WHAT'S GOING ON? And now look around at all your fellow humans. No matter how dulled-out or in a hurry they might be, aren't they still asking, "What is this Life here? This is so amazing! What am I doing? What's going on?" The question asks and asks. Look at each of these faces in the crowd and smile, you know that we all have it back there, that same old question. All of us are that surprised at Life, and that curious about it. We know we can't escape it. We're here. We all got the WHA!

You see children, when you think about it, NO ONE EVER EXPLAINS TO US WHAT LIFE REALLY IS. It just keeps on happening. The fundamentalists tell us to stop listening to the question because they have the Answer. But that is their con job. It is always based on urging us to be afraid of Death. But we WHA! believers were not afraid of Death when we were born—we had just come from whatever that is on the other side. Life wasn't a deal. It was just STRANGE AND STRONG! We committed to it with all we had. We had the faith right away. Somebody give me an Amen?

This question, WHA? WHAT'S GOING ON?, is a strong belief. We're not used to questions being the stuff of belief, but bear with me. Let's look at this carefully. If I'm right, then this is the antidote faith for the fundamentalisms of the multinationals and the doomsday Hard Right. We will have a defense—one that we have long had but may not have noticed against the Fear of Death con job.

What does Saint Henry David mean when he thinks he was a wise child? I mean, was he wise when he was *born*? When Henry David Thoreau wants to have the wisdom he was born with, he means he wishes he still had the wisdom of the question, WHA? WHAT'S GOING ON? The belief that all of us always had and always will.

Before we go any farther, please stand and sing the Marvin Gaye refrain three times.

What's Going On?
What's Going On?
What's Going On?

Amen, we don't need to escalate.

But we're wondering . . . if, when we act with the power of The Question, could that be as strong as our fundamentalist opponent, who has The Answer? As business people stride toward their future, expanding quarterly earnings is their Word of God. Can we oppose these people—and their power—with a question?

If our form of belief is stronger, its application won't truly be spelled out in doctrines. We would have the event-by-event questioning ("What are we all up to?") that we recognize from the campaigns of Gandhi and King and Chavez. Presented with a fortress of laws, guns, embarrassing press, and threats of all kinds, our response would come from taking a moment to listen and to again hear that question in ourselves. As we ALL share the question, we can hear The Question being asked by even our most dangerous antagonists.

How can the fearful fundamentalists be interrupted, flummoxed, returned to their own question, returned to the full blast of their own WHA! We're in for a time of strangeness. Our efforts to stop the Shopocalypse will take unrecognizable forms. We need to be ready, the way a baby is ready at the point of birth for a century of peace, and has such resources to protect so much Life!

This is why the marketing departments are so mesmerized by the Life of a child. The Product Gods and their sales forces spend billions of dollars on their search-and-destroy missions of our earliest life. There are billions now targeted exclusively at kids, whole companies devoted to only three-year-olds. They know that they have to get to The Question early . . .

Amen.

Children, the WHA! Question is asking and asking and asking and let's celebrate the question with the choir. Perhaps our Choir Director, James Solomon Benn . . . Brother James, will you lead us in song?

The Beyond Song

We believe in making more than money . . .
Beyond big debts there's a super value.
A Wal-Mart crushed by a great green storm,
A new town rising from the logos to be born.

We believe beyond the U. S. of A. . . . .
The Prez is embedded like a method actor.
Is he on the set? . . . has the star got his gun?
It's a buddy film with God. You better run.

We believe in praying beyond crusades . . .
Eternal life is not flying all night.
No B–2 Bomber, no high tech attack.
A child on the ground is praying that God back.

When did we start to believe beyond you?
When did the product die on the shelf?
I think you lost when you said—
"There is nothing to love but fear itself."

You said—"Life on earth is a network of terror,
And shopping keeps the demons in the zoo."
Well, it's not that we're young or black or labor,
Until you change, we're the Devil to you.

Until you change, we're the Devil to you.

Time for a seventh-inning stretch. The congregation will please rise!

Let's pray together, like a sloppy Gregorian chant. Just sing it all on the same note. Want to join me? Put your hands together like you're praying, up under your chins. Let's look upward, at the sky.

First, face Wall Street:

We believe in stopping our shopping.
We're starting our believing.

Now turn and face the closest Starbucks:

We believe in stopping our shopping.
We're starting our believing.

Now face the White House:

We believe in stopping our shopping.
We're starting our believing.

And now face your TV:

We believe in stopping our shopping.
We're starting our believing.

Great! Change-a-lujah!

Children, we meet today in the fullness of Summer, bouncing around in our Supernatural Hayride!—the ball of fire is rising over us and we are HOT! And every family and animal and plant is demonstrating a faith in Life, the children and the fruits of our love in all their forms are leaping across the ground. We celebrate our independence and get some fun in the sun. So what's the problem?

Belief. The fundamentalists have one rhetorical device that they use all day long. They say that we are not believers and that they are. Their entire project of consumerism and war depends on this idea.

So all the rest of us are "Anti." All of us. And this includes the Earth too, which has been portrayed as antibusiness lately. We are anticonsumerists, antiwar activists, antifamily . . . we are not Believers.

But we have a faith, don't we children?

When Wal-Mart is kept out of our town, off our highway, out of the county, then we will be called antiprogress. But in our faith our love of Life borders on astonishment—and we would never let a company treat Life that way. So of course we believe in a living wage, health benefits, and safety. We have our faith.

When we preempt the power of the angry Product Gods, and we force the beginnings of Peace, they will lash out at the antiwar protesters, the un-American types, but our Action comes from our belief in the preciousness of Life. We have our faith.

When we rise up to pull the Believer's industries back

from harming the planet, they will be surprised because they are not accustomed to Peace people having Power. The Question that is our bedrock surrounds them.

Children, we very much want Life to make Life. We don't want to survive the adventure of living just so we can say "I cheated Death because God was on my side." We want to survive to keep The Question shining. We have our faith.

WHHAAA—lujah!

And now a reading from the Holy Writ:

A voice from Death, solemn and strange,
in all his sweep and power,
With sudden, indescribable blow—towns drown'd—
humanity by thousands slain,
The vaunted work of thrift, goods, dwellings,
forge, street, iron bridge,
Dash'd pell-mell by the blow—yet usher'd Life continuing on,
(Amid the rest, amid the rushing, whirling, wild debris,
A suffering woman saved—a baby safely born!)
—Walt Whitman

Oh Fabulous Unknown, we know that when you brought us into Life that we were not afraid of Death. May we get back to that now—figure out the presence of Death in our Life—so that we don't force it on others. Old Soul Walt

Whitman, help me pull those Product Gods off the shelf
... Amen.

Life-a-lujah! Death-a-lujah!
Thank you Walt.

AT A CRITICAL MASS BICYCLE RIDE,
WITH SISTER LAURA AND BROTHER QUILTY

I wonder if our brother of Brooklyn, Walt Whitman, would agree that a person dies with the same message for the world as a person cries out at birth. The unconditional commitment to Life by a baby who comes into that light outside mother might be the same commitment that a peaceworker has at the time of going back into Death. I would like to recall a story now, from my life, where I stood for awhile after birth and before Death, and tried to listen.

At the time of the 2004 Republican National Convention in New York City I went through a time of Death. Friends, and friends of friends, were passing away. People in their twenties and thirties, or their nineties. Lots of other friends were in prison, jailed by Republican-led police who couldn't read, or wouldn't read, the Constitution. So we were embarking on a time of slow-motion lawsuits and hushed memorials.

Every day that week of the RNC, I tried to take a long bike ride through the park near my home before going into Manhattan for the puppetry and chanting and die-ins and reenactments of the signing of the Declaration of Independence and performances of long unemployment lines: Peace work. On one of those days, I was peddling through the park and saw that the gate to the Quaker cemetery was left open. Someone was working on the grounds. I had never seen the gate to the war resisters' remains open like this.

I walked in. I found the caretaker down in one of the centuries-old families of bodies, below the gate in a dark swale. The trees here are primeval. It is said that this is the original forest, never logged, one of the few in New York City. The white oaks with their great operatic branches go up and up. I got the generous hand-wave: Yes, I could walk around, and I wheeled my bike up toward higher forests and meadows filled with sunlight.

At the fork in the road, where it divided to go in a circle around the forest and around the graves, I stopped again.

Tiered back into the hill were many dead, whose presence was now becoming the fact of my visit, that unmistakable ruling stillness. Then I noticed a sign, about as tall as me—really a thick totem-pole kind of thing—painted white. Vertical black letters made words down the sides of the pole, and I saw that on the faceted surface of this pole, as I walked around it, were messages in English, French, German, Chinese, Spanish, Hebrew, Indian, and Russian.

"Let Peace prevail on this Earth." That is what it said, with the "Let" on the high end and the "Earth" down near the grass. Then I looked up the hill at the graves, the separate small cemeteries from different "Friends' meetings" in the city, and from different times in history. Hundreds of them up there, old bodies and child's bodies. I became aware of my status in my upright body, steadying my bike with one living hand, this extraordinary living body on loan from some mysterious source.

These people under the grass of this beautiful hill had worked for Peace. They are Friends. They are Quakers. This pole with the eight hopeful prayers came from the authority of all that work. I could feel the hope for Peace down in the minutes of their lives, in each heartbeat, now steadied in the late summer heartbeat of this lovely park. The eight Peace prayers kept repeating as I walked by the names and the years and days.

Then a new feeling swept through me from all this, an unmistakable feeling that this would—I sensed this right away—this would always be here for me to remember. All the Deaths around my community and family in recent weeks had somehow conspired to give the feeling of something terribly wrong in the world. From the Sudan and Chechnya to my neighbors and friends—it all felt that way. And the hopelessness was not exactly the worst of it. There was something darker than your usual hopelessness. There was the feeling that Life actively did not make sense. It was not so much the absence of hope but the presence of good peoples' deaths in a pattern of directed confusion. We were being beaten by Life, surrounded by a reawakened Death, a Death that didn't fit at the end of the Life. These last weeks I'd felt the presence of the demons I never believed in.

But the feeling I had that day—there at the strange language pole on the road through the graves—came from this phrase that these people had agreed to repeat as one-by-one they passed into the hill. Let Peace Prevail On This Earth. The dead Friends were saying this to me in unison. The leafy shadows and pops of sunlight moved back and forth across the grave stones. I could hear them talking, looking up from all their work. Let Peace Prevail On This Earth.

It was one of those thoughts that was waiting a long time. It came through me like a physical aftermath. The

Peace message is spoken by the dead here and also by the living who painted the pole and know that they will go into the Earth here soon. They both speak "Let Peace Prevail" at once. It's an intralife chorus. The faith is: When you live your Life making more Life, Death fits in it, because you didn't cheat Life by making bullets and bombs. Life making Life. The Peaceful Dead have their fully wrought lives continuing in the world, as they rest. They have sent Life out beyond themselves. The living are reading this script, the words looping in and out of the ground.

We can leave this simple wish up in the sun for the living to understand while they pass by. Up here with my bike, I feel the belief in Peace coming up into me. I hear the Friends saying these words. I will say these words, too.

START YOUR OWN WHAT?—
THE REV SITS AND THINKS

~ ~

BUOYED BY SPIRIT ON VENICE BEACH,
SHORTLY BEFORE PARADING IN DISNEYLAND. IN WHITE,
BROTHER JAMES BENN, OUR CHOIR MASTER.

I HAVE LETTERS on my old wooden desk from people with the brave and Oddly Holy hope of starting Stop Shopping churches in their own communities. In a special little stack are three such letters, from Ingemar S. in Atlanta, Vic P. in Seattle, and Maryam in Los Angeles.

Ingemar says his town "cannot stop shopping . . . Atlanta needs a spiritual revival." Maryam says, "I'd like to open a branch of the church in Los Angeles, or see if there is one already here . . . tell me how, please!" Vic P asks, "Have you started your own Bible College?"

I have had conversations like this with people in New York, Ohio, Minnesota, Arkansas, California, Melbourne, Hong Kong, Finland, Sao Paulo . . . Consumerism is everywhere. Alas, there's a Big Box hovering over every healthy neighborhood, and we all want to do something about it. And why wouldn't I want to expand our project? I'm an American, after all: YES! I LOVE THIS! EXPAND! EXPAND! EXPAND! A democratic and international uprising with a sense of humor! Radical gospel singers and doppelbillys marching into supermalls around the globe. It's a

funny coup de grace for the big banks' cruel joke of an economy, and it would be wonderfully confusing to the right-wing
televangelists who keep the consumers praying.

Nonsense, of course. We aren't franchisable, I hope. I
mean, we need to study the theater of Sojourner Truth, Crazy
Horse, the Greenpeace canoe headed for the side of the factory ship, the Yes Men and the Red Revues of Brecht's early
days—and maybe we should study the Church of Stop Shopping, too. We have our innovations. Just as long as the gentle
reader knows that we regard no activism as the "best" or others as "incorrect." We need to fight in many ways, from computer hacking to unpermitted parading to pie-throwing to
gourmet shoplifting for the poor (thinking of the Robin
Hoods in Hamburg) to the large-scale beyond-the-Rockettes
synchronized antiglobalization performances by the workers
in Korea to the songs of Victor Jarra . . . . We believe that we
all help each other, even if we don't seem to be on the same
stage.

Laurie Anderson said once that "[m]ost artists have only
three secrets." Well, ours would be: Spiritual power comes
every which way—and certainly not just from organized religion—a right-wing Evil character like my reverse mentor
Jimmy Swaggart can be appropriated and redeployed as a
spirit catcher that is also comic—Hey, Rush Limbaugh steals
lefty stuff at the drop of a hat . . . why not turn the tables on

him? And that joyous gospel and salsa music is portable. It can make you see the light in nonplaces that are officially dehumanized, freedom-deleted, paved-over, and killed. Like half of our country. And the spirited life can be not only post-religious, it can also be funny, sexy, and have a conscience in a way that is creatively conscientious right now, not from a moral rectitude of centuries ago, but responding to wrecking balls, crooked dollars, and nonsense coming into our communities at this moment. Well, Amen!

Say that Ingemar and Maryam and Vic start "churches" in their three cities. These three efforts could be entirely different from one another and at the same time all could be very powerful. And why is that? Well, these are three different cultures. A shout in one town might be a whisper in the next. Voices carry and visions appear in different ways in different places. And, of course, what kind of public expressors will the three of you array around you? Ingemar might gather dancers whose specialty disorients planning commissions, and Maryam may be ready to invent some yogic meditation against which mall security has no resistance and Vic (of the Bible College) might start a writers' reading series that supports independent bookstores.

How different we may be from one another is clear, but how do we also learn from one another? Many activists are heard of only on the grapevines of the housing projects and gatherings around garden plots in vacant lots, or the spotty local press of the supermallized suburbs, or underground Indy media. We do need more local revolutions to show us their tricks. For instance, more than 200 communities have successfully thrown back Wal-Mart invasions, but apart from Inglewood, California's heroic neighborhood/church/labor struggle, which was filmed in Rob Greenwald's movie, *Wal-Mart: The High Cost of Low Prices*, we really don't know much about these remarkable citizen uprisings. I've heard enough of the folk stories coming out of these pitched battles to know that many people stepped out of their usual boundaries and into sidewalk passion plays, trickster phone campaigns, flesh mobs, or runs for office that seemed vaudevillian and sometimes succeeded.

As we hear these Struggle Stories, floating back through the resistance culture, it sounds to us like some of the campaigns had what we would call Fabulous Worship in them: power prayers and neohootenannies and weird contact improv out in front of City Hall, i.e. going to the CEO's frontyard, contacting shareholders directly, ambushing Planning Commission meetings. Others sound like they went straight at the Lake of Hellfire at the POP (Point of Purchase). Don't misunderstand me, those 200 triumphs had days and nights of boring meetings that you could hardly call song and dance—just long toughing-it-out, sitting at tables with lawyers.

But we know that you Maryam, Ingemar, and Vic—and you the reader sitting there in your pew—you have some world-changing tricks up your pant-leg. We know that you are geniuses who offer a spectrum of performances and prayers that the Devil Fortress Mall simply cannot stop. How many times have I been confronted by a suspicious person in a uniform, eyes squinting, "What are you doing?" to which I reply, "Me? I'm shopping," while I look across the fluorescent Big Box and see dozens of elite antishopping commandos. To store security they are indistinguishable from browsing customers. But listen carefully. They are whispering about how they miss the neighborhood that this Big Box destroyed. They are asking nearby shoppers "Do you know where these things were made?" "Let me tell you what was here on this spot ten years ago!" or "This item is for sale down the street and it's the same price and its Fair Trade. Want me to take you there?"

WE ARE SHOPPING—FOR LOST SHOPPERS!

THE ULTIMATE RETAIL INTERVENTION:
COMMUNITY

Communities cannot be planned, as Celebration, Florida—the Disney Company's failed prefab town—proved. But the good news is that there is a long history of remarkable communities that have risen from political action work. A resistance community has so many superheated gatherings to look to as guides, from the Boston Tea Party crazies to Chief Joseph's Nez Perce to ACT UP to the worldwide community that opposes trade agreements like NAFTA. The social groups created in resistance often become the model for—or are an influential presence on—larger, stable communities that evolve later. The coffee cooperatives in Chiapas, who have some of the spirit of the Zapitistas, resist Starbucks the way that Subcommandante Marcos resists the Mexican ruling class. Another example is the kinds of culture-making that can radiate from the experience of Critical Mass bicycle rides. Here in New York the Critical Mass improvisatory ride/parades are monthly, and out of that bonding (and police-hounding) have come rich networks of intimate cooperation . . . gardens, living communities, art-making, and skill-sharing—i. e., a new economy. Thus, a single brave ritual is the seed of a society that would create a transportation alternative—and a whole lot more.

In the Stop Shopping Gospel Choir, we live together when we are touring, sharing motel rooms and buses and vans. Most of the year we are with one another several times in the course of the week, like the (post-religious) church group that we are. We share the email, the song design meetings, and miles of subway benches. There's the roller-derby-ing, gardening, partying. Life passages with one of us will impact all of us: a birth, illness, birthday, adventurous vacation, loss of a loved one. This "real Life" comes up into the words of the sermons and the melodies of the songs in our Fabulous Worships.

The evolution of our community has been guided by the like-minded friends who invite us to resistance hotspots around the world. We might be picked up at the airport or met at the train station to be led to a supermall construction site. Three or four people will be excitedly downloading the whole resistance story, all talking at once, the narrative tumbling out as we drive and walk toward the site—the five- or seven-year struggle to defend the community is always a hair-raising adventure. Meanwhile, we find that over the course of that struggle our hosts have come to know each other well. A resistance community has taken root. There is nothing like a fierce band of brothers and sisters who have been standing down a Wal-Mart.

We have noticed something surprising—and like I say, unplanned—in our coming together as a performance community. The animating principle of the Church of Stop Shopping—as stated from the beginning when I was alone preaching on the sidewalks of Times Square—was "community defense." Now, ten years later, as so many neighborhoods are completely destroyed, we are also in the visionary business of "community reclamation." When we perform, audience folks see how different we all are—race, gender, age, dance moves, and facial jewelry—as we sing in harmony up there. It's community-as-performance. Yes, we have to think about how we can come together again after the Shopocalypse, after these exhausting years of traffic jams and American Idol and a terrible horizon of wars.

Wow. It is so easy for your preacher to suddenly GO DARK. Somebody give me a Change-a-lujah. Let's start over, nice and gingerly.

> *Those who are willing to sacrifice and be of service have*
> *very little difficulty with people. They know what they are all about.*
> *People can't help but want to be near them. They help them;*
> *they work with them. That's what love is all about.*
> *It starts with your heart and radiates out.*
> CÉSAR CHÁVEZ

> *I have to do good in this club. When I finish my work up here,*
> *I've got to walk through all of you.*
> LENNY BRUCE

Community-as-performance. We see it happen without a script. Many alerted local citizens are seen leaving their homes and coming out into public spaces, where they meet each other, strangers at first, but they enter into new relationships—that mix of routine and mystery. A whole world opens up. It sure is different than staying home watching TV. As Kurt Vonnegut says: "Turn off your TV. It IS the government."

And when we meet out in public, a new governance brews in the space between us. The safety from supermalls that certain lucky places have accomplished is similar to the street corners in Jane Jacobs's writing, where a violent intruder is noticed by people on their stoops, at the fruit stand, waiting at the bus stop. The "cascade of eyes" that she describes is a key urban community creation. But it lives anywhere there is resistance. With this cascade of eyes—how we see each other and keep one another safely watched-over in public places—we must will our vigilant compassion into the overpaved, overlogo-ized nowhere-land where We, The People were only supposed to drive, buy, and die.

The key is: perform ANYWHERE YOU CAN. We have sung in Planning Commission meetings, precinct station houses, at gas pumps, in cemeteries, and generally anywhere there are too many cars or cash registers. Whatever you do and wherever you go, you are building a tradition. Your local activists will come to count on your energy. Some longtime progressive folks might be peevish from your new approach, but most will be relieved that someone is moving beyond the ol' march-'n-rally, chants-'n-signs. (For decades we have not known how to escape our parodies of the sixties.)

Your activism may even attract the attention of a Rudy Giuliani from law enforcement, a politician who wants to whip up puritanical votes at your expense. Well, such opposition will serve to dramatize your political position. Your performance adds that Devil to its narrative—and you proceed. That's how the drama of a performance community has worked since Jesus. Citizens witness the police breaking up highly motivated and nonviolent performers, and everyone senses that the courage is coming from singing together, costuming and dancing—and risking jail together. (Of course, this is when we have chosen to perform *visible* theater. We might want to vanish.)

There is a selfish part to this, too: A healthy community feels so good. Peace work is sensual. There is the joy, the mad talk, the music and sex in the air. Let's be a bunch of humans making ourselves into a bunch of humans who agree to bunch a lot more. The computers do not come close to replicating the ferocious fractalization of such a pool of personalities. Our choir keeps us in a state of head-whipping-around, jaw-dropping surprise. (Today, as I sit here in Brooklyn at my old desk, the choir phone-called, faxed, and emailed 102 news desks here in New York for a march on Victoria's Secret. Just unbelievable. Mara Luna Rivas just called me. She's a single mother of a handsome boy, Mason, and the daughter of one of the East Village hero-poets, Bimbo Rivas. She's been on the phone with what I would have presumed were the Bill O'Reilly worshippers at the news desk of the *New York Post*, talking about global warming and clear-cutting!)

If you talk to people who were there at a crucial time of change—say the ones who rode the buses in Freedom Summer—the relationships are the stuff of their memories. The deepness that friendship develops when centuries of prejudice are releasing the very worst that humanity has to offer, and you and your friends are marching right at this together . . . that's the energizing thing. It is why so many people stay in even the most discouraging social-change work.

It is also what our opponents fear the most. They accused the labor organizers and the civil rights workers of every sin under the sun. What would seem like the very personal persecutions of Lenny Bruce, Paul Robeson, Sacco and Vanzetti, the lynchings and the public slanders and McCarthyism—it always had a community attack within it. The bohemian gatherings around Bruce were scary to fifties official America. Robeson inspired paranoid fears of a communist uprising of the children of slaves. Much of this Salem witch-hunt-style violence came from the fear of coherent communities.

Today, the multinational marketers understand the power of community, and try to manufacture a docile and indebt kind of consumer citizenry while simultaneously attacking the communities of conscience. They attempt to do this with precision marketing that persuades us that we don't need to organically build our gatherings anymore. They say: "Why trust strangers? We'll prescreen everyone you meet. Yes, they all buy the same things as you—and that means they're safe. At least you can stand in line with them! We will help you *purchase* yourselves into a community."

There was a time when you heard theories about how branding together was the same as bonding together. Professor James Twitchell wrote books arguing that the person who buys a GAP t-shirt in Paris at the same moment as someone buying a GAP t-shirt in San Diego—that these two folks were somehow in a community together. Unbelievably enough, this was a sexy theory for awhile. But let preacher suggest what's really sexy: Two browsers who are standing at the same display refuse to buy a sweatshop product together, and then turn and speak directly.

Talking and listening (and singing!) directly. Start it there, with real contact on the ground. Hearing without a cell. Looking into your eyes. DIRECT BODY MEDIA. Then let the long distance communities flow from that. But—why would they try to change something as ordinary as talking and listening? Well, no telling how we might get together. In the coalitions who have resisted Wal-Mart, you're apt to see a third-generation Republican hardware store owner standing next to a lesbian bookstore proprietor. Then later you'll see them march together against the war. *They really talked.* Once, in Lawrence, Kansas, I saw an older couple square dancing to hip hop on a blaster. It was the Public Enemy classic, "It Takes a Nation of Millions to Hold Us Back." Now that's a fine church!

LET'S BACK AWAY FROM THE PRODUCT

If you bring forth what is within you,
what you bring forth will save you. If you do not bring
forth what is within you, what you do not
bring forth will destroy you.

—JESUS CHRIST, THE GOSPEL OF THOMAS

"Backing Away From The Product" is our main practice, the same thing in our Stop Shopping world as "sitting" is for the Buddhists. (Wait a minute, do Buddhists sit? Perhaps you the reader, at this very moment, are a sitting Buddhist.) Moving along, when we back away—literally reach out for, even hold, pause, and then retreat—from a product, or an advertisement, or a cash register, then the magic happens. The soul and the body do a double take as the addiction is lifted. That's when all the stuck stuff can move. Consumerism congeals our insides, imprisons our godsightings, slows our 714 stories down. When the signal comes in that the way is clear, all sorts of experiences—dreams and traumas and glories—rise up.

Getting out of product-life is like meeting yourself again. Just sitting here typing about it, I pause as a personal movie switches on, playing a memory of South Dakota, when I was a kid in the early sixties. I'm standing in a dark backyard watching a satellite go over and thinking that Cape Kennedy threw it over the prairie. That's the memory media package I just saw. The feeling of it is like high quality chocolate, slightly bitter and so lovely. This is like the retrieval of a genome coded as imagery, something that came into a buck-toothed kid's body that got swept away later, as I grew up moving from city to city.

It'll be different for you, but the same, too. We have learned in the Church of Stop Shopping that memory recla-mation is key, then sharing and comparing. The overheated economy shoots its imagery at all of us—the young espe-cially. This has happened in some form to everyone for years. We are stuffed with the fabricated dreams of ads, the corny Hollywood fictions, and now our own stories are blocked down in our intestines. This is how they make us con-sumers, slowed down in a swooshing world. When the cap is off, and we are free of product-life, we're suddenly streaming with our own media. The memory from South Dakota? It must have been waiting down in my left foot. I hadn't remembered it in twenty years.

Personal revelation is as necessary as public revolution. "Backing Away From The Product" has to be both a spiritual practice and a public embarrassment so extreme that its wit-nesses won't stop talking about it for years. Amen? AMEN!

The whole change-theory of our faith is that if enough of us Back Away at once, things will get better. What happens during this supposedly Un-American withdrawal, as our fingers release from the product, and the product looks at us with such disappointment and dismay? What goes on during this rejection of one thing and acceptance of another is the whole point. We always knew that there was more to this "Backing Away From The Product" than your average boycott. In completing the cycle, we are letting that lodestone of startlingly personal programming rise up, come into our gestures and faces, and move out into the social world beyond.

One of the ways in which we are so sure that there is power in Backing Away is that police and journalists and their camera people come running with such dedication when we practice it. We don't even have to sing and preach to cause an uproar. The products themselves seem to know. All the surveillance comes alive, the red phones ring, the whole military operation of retail trips its wire. But it is also in the people! Why on our Shopocalypse tour across America were those crowds in the Mall of America so engrossed with the Stop Shopping anthem echoing through their Abercrombie & Fitch?

I would hazard this guess. For lots of reasons (all the violence, for one), fundamentalism doesn't have the attraction it once had. In the Mall of America, the main stage was empty and we got up there and sang "Stop Shopping." The way people gathered—they were feeling an unbuyable joy. In themselves as well as from us. The world beyond the monochromatic utopias of products and god-sellers—it's the WHA! Question—it's more fun!

A little help from your friends . . . helps a lot. The joy felt when Backing Away together, when deep in a mall and Backing Away, is personal and social in equal measure. It's amazing how vast that landscape is when the product, the occuption force, finally leaves. That's when we can really move in. The ghosts of the independent shops or the family farms or the songbirds in the wetlands that existed on the land beneath the mall—we wait for it to come up through. We are filling up and moving in as we Back Away.

When the Stop Shopping Gospel Church was doing missionary work in Bentonville, Arkansas, we spent time in the cemetery in back of Wal-Mart's world headquarters. We were gathering the Life that was in that place, singing names from the gravestones before circling the headquarters and focusing our concentrated voodoo vaudeville at the front door of the building. A Big Box always has Life and lives buried under it. We have to learn to recall the lost hopes and dashed dreams of so many unreported, uncomplaining citizens. The Placelessness of the Big Box is replacing a Place, and the Life is still there to be honored. Each of our bodies is a place too, and my dead are rising . . . YOU TOO?

This sensing of the submerged communities, exploded neighborhoods, families fleeing not just joblessness and crime but also miles of confusing emptiness, the modern architecture of slabs and dust and ads—this has a lot to do with starting our kind of Church. When old-timers are suddenly forced into a trailer park somewhere, we need to hear what they have to say. We need those details in our radical art. We're ripping open this camouflaging of our personal past and our immediate neighbors. The multinationals advance toward us with fusillades of white noise, endless repetitions of sound and sight. We resist by bringing back the human details and building our lives moment by moment. Be quiet. Back Away from the product. Our own voice is coming back, we feel our personal past re-arriving.

We are staring back at the product and we are seeing the Life and lives of others submerged behind the packaging. Somehow knowing our own details helps us recognize the human faces looking out at us from some hidden sweatshop or toxic, hot afternoon in the product's past. Suddenly we feel the vision-movie of the labor that created that product, that was displaced from this land, and the metals and earth-blood that are under the glossy surface of the vaccuwrap. When we Back Away from the product, all kinds of Life rushes back in.

WHERE TWO OR THREE BACK AWAY:
THE MOTHER OF ALL RETAIL INTERVENTIONS

You enter a Big Box or a chain. Fan out through the store until each member of the congregation is standing opposite a product that they have personally felt drawn to.

You each stand there in the Devil's retail environment and raise your hand. Wrap your fingers around the neck of the product you have chosen. Lift it lovingly off the shelf and pull it to your bosom, as if to suckle.

Walk down the aisle toward the check-out counter in that great American migration, the journey to the purchase. Clutching the product to your heart, in that eternal Mother-Mary-and-child gesture—you finally arrive. You stand, in our culture's most prominent public ritual, addressing the back-side of the person in front of you. Yes, you are now IN LINE.

Now you go into your brand reverie. You recall your Life with this bottle of perfume, this tie, this Tonka Toy, this sneaker. This is your buddy, the product. You adore it, and it's good-naturedly putting up with you. You even forgive the product its more annoying characteristics: the label, the bar code, the plastics, the packaging, the price. There it all is—take the good with the bad. You continue to hold it, fondly. The product loves you, too, after all.

Now you are close to the swiping moment, and the bagging finale. Assert yourself now. Make your product obey.

Insist on something that the product resists. Demand that you get the facts, a bit of a background check on this sexy product that's come into your Life with such panache. If you're facing a flavor-saving genetically engineered tomato, for instance, then let the fake red swell in your eye. Sure, go ahead, have your love moment, but then discover the nightmare world behind the red rotundity. Dig up the dirt. Ask that tomato, "Where the hell did you come from?"

The product will deny that there ever was anyone else, that its Life started with you, always and forever sitting on that shelf waiting for your hand. The product will say, "I have no past. I am only yours."

But you already picture the box of tomatoes, unloaded from a truck. Yes the tomato was shipped by fossil-fueled trucks and boats and planes from the other side of the globe and here it is in your hand. Its red steroid tomato cells are in parade formation, obedient and marching in lock step, ready to do your bidding. Your hand is on it, but there is a long shadow of burning gas and oil, of CO_2 exhausts. There are the people in the tomato fields, who are paid what? There are the pesticides and herbicides they inhale. This movie is projected inside your fingers. Now your relationship is becoming strained, the product feels stuck in your hand, trapped, because you KNOW.

You are an American consumer, and you have trusted this product. You hold it next to your heart. You face the cash register, and the line of consumers also caught in the swoon of stunning brightness and Muzak. But suddenly there is only you. The counter person wants to scan the tomato and holds out a hand.

Now is the moment. Do the following and believe.

1. Laugh out loud. Say, "I'm sorry I forgot my money!"
2. Turn and return the product to its place. You must ignore the product's initial flush of sadness, followed by its anger as it seethes with betrayal.
3. As you release your fingers and step three steps back, OWN this separation. You are now entering the Heaven of your new community.
4. Turn toward the door and move into public space. Retake that public space, with no product in your hand. You ARE part of the public, even though you have refused to buy.
5. Exit the store and meet your friends at a prearranged spot, the parking lot, someone's home, a nearby forest, and have your Fabulous Worship.

The Fabulous Worship of your church is the performance of your first postcommercial thoughts. It is whatever your group creates together at this point. It is the improvisation that becomes formal high ritual the moment it happens. All is forgiven ahead of time. You can laugh the whole time. Maybe you never stopped laughing from the moment you returned your product. Freedom's a funny thing.

We do recommend that your church form a circle with the members facing inward. These are sacred things, these postcorporate revealings. Whatever form the performance takes, however comic or teary, however clumsy or surreal or even ordinary feeling—let it come.

There is no time expectation, or limit. It can be over very quickly and that is fine, but my suggestion is that you let it go forward and go through periods of silence. Let the whole thing go longer than you expect. Again, there are no mistakes. Maybe it will feel boring or weird or ho-hum. Believe me, it's all Miraculous. You are starting a culture without a corporation. This is very exciting but you may have feelings you don't recognize at first.

I would like to suggest a few approaches that we have explored:

Say that there are three of you. As you walked out of the store, perhaps across the parking lot to your prearranged meeting spot, each of you had your first postproduct thoughts.

The product's erotic pull is waning, it is farther and farther into the distance, back there in the glowing retail emporium. Inevitably, as you walk away, some first image, thought, dream, memory of the past, or vision of the future rises. An entire story may unfold in front of you while you walk.

And now you are holding your friends' hands. Unmediated by any interloping product, you are face to face with your neighbors in the flesh. And as you hold these hands and face these faces, you hold also the memory of that first post-product thought.

Trust that you can share this revelation, no matter what it is, no matter how unimportant it may feel, it is a God-sighting.

Here's a sample prayer:

Oh Fabulous Unknown—creator of laughter, evolution and revolution—protect us as we reveal our post-product visions. And, all the Life blasted from this field by this pavement and this Big Box, and all the shopkeepers and unhurried local characters, please be with us in our attempt bring you back, as we rise from the Big Box ourselves. . . . Amen.

For our Holy Demo, we offer a transcription from a tape we made in a recent parking lot Fab Worship, starring our friends Oona, Merc, and Charley. Here's what they reported, after escaping the fiery lake of Shopping Hell.

OONA: I was walking out of those electronic doors, and the sun hit me, and I walked out into these cars here and my first thought was: Oh, I'm gonna float up over all this. This sea of cars and SUVs—I feel like I can fly up over them. I mean, walk over them, like the ground was up over the tops of all the cars. I just walked up on a grassy hill over the cars. People from inside the store and inside the cars were, I saw them come up on the grass with me, and the ground was up over the cars as far as we could see. Everyone was lying around in the grass, or walking and running. Long grasses, windy and sunny. (pause) That's it.

They all say: Fabulous Unknown, thanks for the advertising-free community access programming.

MERC: Well, my thought started when I was laughing at the cash register there. The counter girl was flirting so heavily with the bagger boy that the—this was the whole story for me. (laughter) My emotional connection with the product was, well, my product was this bar-b-que thing set—it knew our relationship was over. I was more interested in . . . in those kids, and they were laughing with me. And I'm sure it was all against the rules and caught on the surveillance. Anyway, so when I was leaving the store, I had these memories of the first time I was slow dancing with a girl, in junior high. And were were dancing and it felt good. I was a fourteen-year-old virgin at the time (laughter) and just the dancing was about as much as I could take. Her name was Linda Pieken. I felt her heat coming through her white dress. And her face had a quality like she was staring at something so I followed her eyes and looked around and we were surrounded by kids who were . . . maybe they were slow-dancing at some point earlier but now they were all necking on the chairs and couches . . .

you see, this was someone's parent's rec room. They were all kissing, in front of each other. Wow. Oh, this is one of those necking parties I always heard about. So, Mary and I looked back at each other. We stopped dancing. She was taller than me. And we stood there and I was terrified, of course. And she laughed suddenly and put her hands on my face.

Everyone: Fabulous Unknown, thanks for the advertising-free community access programming.

CHARLEY: Well, when I cam out of that sales hole, I felt like they were watching me. I felt the cameras on me. And I don't think I ever got to my own thoughts, really. The security people, the cameras, the conversations on their radios. When I put my basketball back, the basketball called the police—that's what it felt like. Cuz all the way back here across the parking lot, I felt like eyes were on me. Like I'm being watched right now as we stand here. Don't you think the surveillance cameras up on those light posts there—someone is watching three weird people holding hands? Maybe they can hear us, too, I don't know. I feel like I'm a target. So I'm sorry my big thought after getting out . . . it's paranoid and fucked up . . .

We repeated: Fabulous Unknown, thanks for the advertising-free community access programming.

Then I asked Oona and Charley and Merc to share their

post-product thoughts again, but let the stories mix together in one big story. So they tried this, still holding hands . . . talking over each other.

Help us God that is Not A Product—with our big replacement story. Strange-a-lujah.

OONA, MERC, and CHARLEY by turns: . . . walking in that grassy field. . . . the grassy hill that buries the cars . . . necking, kissing, and necking on . . . there are open rec rooms up there . . . old couches and . . . but no televisions . . . what are we doing . . . strolling with all the products and cars buried far below us . . . the three products we put back on the shelves are very pissed . . . we put them back but they got out and now . . . they soar over us like eagles . . . metal surveillance eagles . . . well they know we aren't buying anything anymore . . . got to keep their eye on us . . . intelligence-gathering eagle drones . . . paid for by developers and . . . I'm fourteen again and those parents can't possibly come back into that basement! They can't come back and ruin the party . . . what? what are you talking about? (laughter) Because the grassy hill is rolling over the products . . .yeah, keeps 'em away . . . keeps the metal computer-brained eagles away . . . we'll let 'em watch, though . . . the grassy paradise is coming out of that kissing . . . what? . . . sure . . . the grassy hill is coming out of the . . . coming out of the . . . well, all that slow dancing

(laughter) . . . kissing brings down the surveillance eagles . . .
we bring them down to the grassy rec room . . . what? . . . and
. . . and what . . . and they turn into actual lonely people . . .
three lonely people who . . . (laughter) hold hands like us . . .
and . . . (laughter)

Amen! Change-a-lujah!

REV'S POST-SCRIPT: Oona, Charley, and Merc made one story
out of their three stories, and the imagery, language, and that
new love-logic at the end—good job. The earth rolling over the
pavement, the lovers walking up over it into the sun, and the
grass, and the products refusing to give up, replacing the birds,
hovering overhead in the form of intelligence-gathering drones
and then pulled down into the change. Sensuousness and
laughter overtaking the techno-fear, and it is selling . . . nothing! (And it seems like paranoid Charley felt better by the end.)

Now our Holy Demo went in this one direction this time,
but if you try the Mother of All Retail Interventions—god
knows what you'll end up with. Whatever you've got as your
God-sightings mix, you have started a new economy. When I
say economy I mean new juice, new meaning, new faith—
items in our present currency are only measured as profit
centers.

The bravery that rises up in your non-commercial air-
church in the parking lot is exactly what the multi-nationals

fear the most. With a set of images and meaning coming from outside their system, you can return to express yourself with the intensity of this new intimate economy. You might return to that big box as a dance company that re-choreographs shopping gestures to devastating effect, or a debating society invisibly camouflaged in local dialects, or how about a secret employee taking your God-sightings inside . . .(Maybe Charley could work security in that mall and make films out of parking lot anti-consumerist neo-pagan rituals he catches on his surveillance system.)

Yes, the Don't Disturb The Customers is just amusing now. Now, anything can happen. The advancing wall of eminent domain, chains and big boxes, privatized commons—that wall is made of fear and advertising, that's all. We have inside ourselves, and the Place still has inside it, a counter-vision of far greater strength. Citizen's groups we've known and loved have this mix of memory and playful vision when they save a town, or stop a war, or let a field of sumac and gooseberries save us!

THE FALL SERVICE

The Place-a-lujah! Devotions,

OR

Stop Shopping, Start Freedom

—•—

House, patch of meadow, oh evening light
Suddenly you acquire an almost human face
You are very near us, embracing and embraced.

RAINER MARIA RILKE

"TRAFFIC-JAMMING"—PREACHING AND SINGING
(AND LEAFLETING WHEN WE CAN GET PEOPLE TO ROLL
DOWN THEIR WINDOWS) ABOUT GLOBAL WARMING
TO THE SOULS LOST IN CARS. THIS ACTION'S
IN SAN FRANCISCO.

PPLACE-A-LUJAH!

Welcome Children, to our Commons, our Place, our stage, our street corner. In today's sermon let's get together and do some city planning. We want to go find those imitations of our Places. You know—where they take the style of our Main Street, suck it into a big box, and then invite us to come in and shop, figuring that we're longing for our old Life, the one that they stole. Let's accept those invitations, go to the centers of the supermalls and Reclaim our Commons. Amen?

Let Us Pray:

> We ask the God that has no advertising campaign—
> please bless us with Strategically Inappropriate Behavior.
> We gotta be Surreal! We gotta be Exorcised! We gotta be
> Impossible! Put on our raucous First Amendment selves!
> Bless us with the unexpected language and gesture wor-
> thy of the Commons we hope to reclaim. Oh lordy, give
> us the instruction manual for the FOOL TOOL.
> Amen.

May I preach now?

Children, I've always been drawn to a movement that barely has a name. Sometimes it appears as a double negative, as if it is beyond shame, like you can't face it directly. I am talking about the "Anti-Displacement Movement."

Generally, it goes like this—we say NO, WE AINT MOVING when the very big institutions insist we do just that. With every member of any local chapter of the Church of Stop False Eminent Domain, we hear egregious stories. Here in New York we could talk about how the Hakim family and their grill was in the lobby of the Selwyn Theater for three decades, but then got kicked when the theater got changed to the American Airlines Theater. A mortal sin! Or—there is a sordid history everywhere—we could talk about the Torres family of the Esperanza Garden in the East Village, who found their garden sold by Rudy Giuliani to one of his campaign contributors for a cut rate.

Now, I know every one of you in the congregation is thinking right now of an instance of local Placefulness pulled into Placelessness.

We have all felt the tearing feeling, the pain of people pulled from a Place that was filled with meaning. Families getting pushed around by big money—an unfortunate American tradition. This is accompanied by demonizing finger-pointing at neighborhoods: "blighted," "crime area," "under-used." It is the developer's old con: I am the Future and you are not. My skyscrapers, malls, chain stores, and gated communities are shiny, made of metal, glass, and sky. The people who live here are shiny too. Now, I ask you: That's the Future that we're shamed into? There's a bit of dust on that shine—since that kind of living is surveilled, hushed, secretly financed, conspicuous, tended to by minimum wage security folks, and has a bad carbon footprint.

This city planning features the disappearance of people talking in small, jumpy, laughing scenes—the good chaos in parks and streets. There might be a little less litter in these new spaces (or not), but there's a lot less people. Rilke's "embrace" is nowhere to be found.

Bumper sticker alert!

GENTRIFICATION IS THE ABSENCE OF GOD.

Amen?

Today, let's build a Church of Place, a praying Place, a dreaming Place, an embracing Place. This is being "at home," where God-sightings come up out of us and allow us to look out at the world without mediation. This is the public Place where we are allowed to carry unsponsored visions and blow them out into the public air, crossing into one another, mixing our private dreams and ordinary neighborhood hellos.

This hot, complex human living is jealously sought after by ad departments, sales reps, and developers, and we are then constantly forced to move, as they mine the warmth we leave behind until that mine is empty.

And now the Reading of the Word. Now be patient with this language, you know much religious literature can be hard to understand sometimes. This is a translation from the French.

And all the spaces of our past moments of solitude,
the spaces in which we have suffered from solitude, enjoyed,
desired and compromised solitude, remain indelible within us, and
precisely because the human being wants them to remain so.
We know instinctively that this space identified
with our solitude is creative . . .

GASTON BACHELARD

Ah yes, solitude.

I want to be alone.
GRETA GARBO

Sunday School Lesson: Remember back when you were seven, eight, or nine years old. Remember a Place that you would go to when you were just starting to think of Life as something that would be different for you than for other people. It might have been an attic or up on the roof or down at a vacant lot on the corner or on your grandmother's porch or up in a tree. You would go there alone and just look out at Life. Did you have a Place like this? Place-a-lujah!

You weren't necessarily trying to get away from your parents. This wasn't a rebellion, necessarily, but it was you and you alone. You would sit there and have . . . thoughts . . . Dreams . . . images. Sometimes with a loved thing, like an old book, a doll, or a little box. Maybe you looked up at the starry night. And looking out and trying to grasp the whole of Life, you thought of the unexperienced years of your Life waiting promisingly before you, out there ahead of you, as vast and unexplained as the stars of the night sky above you. The universe is just too mysterious to fathom, and yet there you are, in your Place, just beginning your conscious Life, knowing surely that you are special.

In our Stop Shopping services we have been asking people to remember their Place. We turn up the lights and I walk out there with the microphone offered, Jerry Springer-style, and we hear things like: "I would go into the attic, in all the old musty family stuff, sit there by the window. Where my brothers couldn't find me," or "the bottom of the deep end of the swimming pool," or "there was a willow tree in back, and I'd sit under the swaying branches and wonder about things." That's a phrase that I hear a lot, "I wonder about things . . ." It really means "I feel out the Unknown"—an experience best felt in solitude.

We start ourselves in these Places. Humming a little tune, looking up at the sky. We start our identities. We start leaving some stories in and other stories out. We've talked about one of the key teachings of the church, that we are each made of 714 stories. Well, this is where we begin to anthologize.

There is a straight line from that solitude to a good friendship.

When a friend shouts your name in greeting and runs toward you, full of excitement and recognition, what's happening at that moment? That whole feeling, that look on the face—that friend is recollecting, in a flash, all your *stories* and they rise to excite his or her own stories. Meeting a friend is really complex. When you walk up to me, I release hundreds of memories that remind me of you—observations, songs, tidbits, temperatures, films, people you resemble, the swoop of your lower back, photographs that fell out of books that had nothing to do with you but remind me of you some-how—all that stuff surfaces and adds up to a composite of you that is so unlike anyone else, it's breathtaking! Friend! That concoction of the two of us, the ability to DO that starts in our childhood place. All our stories light up from those two manifold memories, in our two faces.

And, of course, friends make community.

> *If you meet a stranger in your neighborhood three times,*
> *then the third time, make it a matter of principle that you will hail*
> *that stranger and exchange names. We build neighborhoods consciously.*

SAMUEL "CHIP" DELANY

The flow of stories to the surface between two or three, and then ten and thirty, in a park, on the corner, in a diner, or climbing up a path in the woods—talking and sharing and re-creating. This is how we evolve. Positive change rarely comes from the policies handed down from Power. We need the mutating humor, the fearless invention of a healthy Commons.

There was a time when there were fields in the centers of towns, where people dismounted and loafed, hitched wagons, the strings and the reeds of musical instruments were ready to go—for money, for love, to waste time. Pickpockets, tap dancers, laughter and worry, relatives spying on young ones, cads seducing, traders trading—and everyone but the tax collector was cursing the King. The thing the Commons areas in history ALL had was an agreement by people to act and talk outside of Power.

Nowadays, we catch our culture-making on the run, because a hologram of the King sits in the park covered with surveillance cameras. The King can't be alone! Or I should say, The Corporation can't be alone, because any place that is not owned or licensed is eyed suspiciously, considered "underdeveloped." They are trademarking the water and the air, the radio frequencies and the cyber portals, the forests on the horizon and the street corner to the left of our front door. It feels hopeless sometimes. Let's start to defend ourselves right where we live.

It has come to this: *We are called extremists if we want a healthy neighborhood.* We resist by taking personal control of our personal stories, walking freely and maybe loudly, demanding clear and quick access to our pasts, our lives, our friends. We resist by not being in cars, by knowing the history of our neighborhoods: where the Underground Railroad safe houses took in the runaway slaves, where some prophetic character defined everything from a table in a tavern. (In my neighborhood that person would be . . . Walt Whitman! Lucky neighborhood!)

And always, we want to know the first names of all the people in our neighborhoods.

We have a responsibility right now to create more Commons. We meet one another on the street and we are too often cloaked. Perhaps because we are the subjects of consumerism, we cannot show to the public air our original selves. We are in a hurry, exhausted, worn down. Or we are giving out signals that are too predictable and fashionable, not surprising—we are simply sinking into a larger dominant culture: toting a cell phone, iPod, magazine to hide behind as WE PRETEND TO BE EXTRAS FROM DAWN OF THE DEAD. How can we Reclaim the Commons if we build a wall around our head?

Well, this is a conservative time, and there is a deadliness—which is tricky and can feel like safety—in mimicking the monster. It's easier to ride iPodded and mildly anesthetized. Our Church of Stop Shopping always pastes our Reverend Billy posters over the famous shadow dancers of the iPod ads when we see them on the street. Because if we, as communities, don't break out of that sinister corporatization of the body—that's the Death of Place, PERIOD. We have to break out of the iPod ads. Will you join us? Let's burst out of those billboards and *really dance in the streets.* PLACE A LUJAH!

Oh, the choir needs to testify. Is there a soloist who wants to shout it out!? Tell us what we gotta be sometimes! Impossible!

> *I see Peace hit the talking heads like amazing facial tics.*
> *I see orangutans debating the mahogany loggers.*
> I got to be Surreal sometimes to understand!

I see the plain truth rising like a fifties Japanese lizard.
I see rec rooms devour Rupert Murdoch in front of his sons.
I got to be Exorcised sometimes to understand!

I see new drug laws that give prosecutors no time to play with.
I see the fine print open wide like a prison door.
I got to be Impossible sometimes to understand!

You see the Starbucks Mermaid got her nipples back.
You see fake bohemians swallowed by your sidewalks.
You got to be Surreal sometimes to understand!

You see tourists walk backwards out of their own pollution.
You see them go home and demand a local paradise.
You got to be Exorcised sometimes to understand!

You see the Stock Exchange paying for itself for once.
You see the CEO cannot cash his welfare check.
You got to be Impossible sometimes to understand!

We see Goofy and Jerry Falwell in the O.K. Corral.
We see the battle of the disastrous religions.
We got to be Surreal sometimes to understand!

We see the Pentagon wake up from its video games.
They see the whistling shrapnel isn't pixilated.
We got to be Exorcised sometimes to understand!

We see the president didn't have to stand naked after all.
But he does see the children he killed singing on his Teleprompter.
We got to be Impossible sometimes to understand!

Let Us Pray,

Fabulous Unknown, mother and father of all Commons,
may we shake our hips out of our consumer shadows,
shed the wires and air-brushed erogenous zones, and take
back the old grassy center of town. Let's meet there and
dance, and let the new beliefs fly! Place-a-lujah!
    Amen.

> *The people have the power.*
> PATTI SMITH

> *The lead character of any novel is the reader.*
> *The lead character of any play is the audience.*
> KURT VONNEGUT

Ms. Smith and Señor Vonnegut are resisting the hero
role that we want to assign them. They are on the stage but
they are pointing at us. It's up to us now.

The First Amendment is our helpmate.

When Ground Zero here in New York was converted into
the opposite of a Commons, we were thrown back into a

strange position. We became an audience that had to sit
there as violence grew from the initial tragedy, and nearly
every one of us had duct tape over our mouths. New Yorkers
were not even cast as extras in the action thriller that we had
created with our blood. We were told to stay away from
Ground Zero, which grew a rough silvery-gray prison fence
around it, fourteen feet high.

At the Church we prayed over the crisis, discussed it, and
lapsed back into uneasy silence. Finally, we lit on an action.
We posted this invitation on the Church site.

> Every Tuesday, down in the World Trade Center train sta-
> tion inside Ground Zero, we will start reciting the First
> Amendment—"Congress Shall Make No Law . . . "—into
> our cell phones. At 6:30 p.m. we will begin to repeat the
> Amendment again and again and we will do this until
> 7:00 p.m. Then we plan to gather and sing it together
> rhythmically in a circle.

Let's all say this together, children. We should recite this
single sentence, in one big breath, every day. Are you ready?
INHALE, AND:

> Congress shall make no law respecting an establishment
> of religion, or prohibiting the free exercise thereof; or
> abridging the freedom of speech, or of the press; or the

right of the people peaceably to assemble, and to petition
the Government for a redress of grievances.

We are working on exercising the First Amendment
right of free speech and peaceable assembly. We feel that
Ground Zero needs to be a working Commons in our community, and an international village square in the world.
Because people from all over the planet are there every day,
gawking from a sentimental distance. Bring them down the
steps into the sacred pit, where the Wall Street commuters
descend to get their train back to Jersey. We need to be able to
share our memories of 9/11 and have our outspoken opinions and shout them out—you know, like Americans.

The people who we enticed into Ground Zero on Tuesdays, who were from other countries and cultures, often said
that they never knew the First Amendment, but they often
felt it in the *personality* of Americans. In that way they knew it
was there. The single sentence with the five freedoms, written by James Madison and Thomas Jefferson, is an extraordinary, messy, scary way to organize a society. It guarantees
freedoms and trusts that people will find their way.

Every challenge to the First Amendment, starting with
the Sedition Act in 1798, then the Espionage Act in 1914,
and, of course, Jim Crow laws, exploits fear. Freedom is
banned because of the threat of the unknown, of the for-

eigner, of real people. The Bush administration truly seemed to hate the First Amendment. Senator Robert Byrd pointed out that in their public documents they couldn't bring themselves to give the U.S. Constitution a capital "C."

The First Amendment is kept alive the way it has always been kept alive. Citizens dramatize the logical or illogical extremes of it. They put the Odd back in that God. The public and the courts are pushed into an adjustment to the force of Free Speech, and so they reaffirm the Bill of Rights. No, Officer, the World Trade Center train station is not private property. Yes, Officer, this is the grassy center of town and my 714 stories are coming up into the public eye. No, Officer, this is not a threat. Sometimes you have to be surreal or nothing makes sense. Yes, Officer, this is a town-cry, this is our solitude, this is our announcement of the legal entertainment of tomorrow! Yes, Officer, we know this is hallowed ground.

Yes, the First Amendment is our permit.

And yes, the United States is our Place.

THE SHOPOCALYPSE TOUR

CONFESSIONS ACROSS AMERICA

THE CHOIR CALMS DOWN CONSUMPTION IN THE
MALL OF AMERICA. FROM LEFT WE HAVE FRENCH BEN,
SHANNON, QUILTY (IN THE GLASSES) ... SPOOKILY
SINGING *SHOPOCALYPSE*.

MEMBERS IN GOOD STANDING of the Church of Stop Shopping and those interested in the Church are encouraged to write to Reverend Billy at www.revbilly.com with confessions, good news, and other relevant correspondence. The following messages were received while on The Shopocalypse Tour, which kicked off with forty singers and musicians departing from New York in two bio-diesel buses. After a robust Buy Nothing Day in Times Square, they traveled west across the U.S., into the shopping frenzy. After thirty days and thirty nights of adventures, including a bus–truck accident, unpermitted parades down the Magnificent Mile, the Mall of America, and Wal-Mart headquarters in Bentonville, and a tent revival in Lubbock, Texas, the final push to slow down the shopping season saw the church's surprise participation in Disneyland's Christmas Day Parade.

Dear Reverend,

I invented a super high-powered chemical-dye laser that will paint corporate logos on the new moon, so at night the whole world will see Coca-Cola or IBM painted on the moon.

—Gregory, Florida, MA

Dear Gregory,

Right, and the next step is to make the moon a point of purchase, so that each person can see products there and access a simple touch-screen order form located in the Sea of Tranquility. That's about as incredible as what we're doing over the next weeks. I'm writing from Sammy the Bus, and we're on the George Washington Bridge now. We're off to America, on a mission to save Christmas from the Shopocalypse. The choir is very happy, can't stop singing. Going right into that shopping frenzy . . . Thanks for the scary joke, it builds up our resistance muscles.

—Rev

Dear Rev,

I have learned of a great evil brewing in the heart of our very neighborhood, from what I hear the whore of Babylon is trying to set up shop and erase a glowing symbol of freedom. BR Guest restaurant chain is planning to buy the Pyramid Club on Ave A in New York City. I hope this is only Satan tempting me with hallucinations of the Shopocalypse, but I fear it may be true. BR Guest is owned by Mickey and Goofy!

—Brother Nico, NY, NY

Dear Brother Nico,

Disney is buying the Pyramid?! I shouted this aloud here and caused the rockers in the bus to start moaning. Maybe we should turn the busses around and come right back. We're in Jersey now. Already pummeled by the steady drum beat of identical details. The highway has got logo after logo after logo . . . . My god—all across the country? Can we do this? Alright Nico, there will be no second Pyramid Club if that one disappears. You can't replace the rock-n-roll dust caked on the silver walls in that back room. Nico, this is the holy of holies, the inner sanctum, and a national treasure.

Yes Nico, we'll come and preach and sing in the Pyramid's defense if you call us in. By the way, check out "Critique of the Pyramid" by Octavio Paz. In Mexico there is the developed nation and the undeveloped nation. The developed nation forces its idea of development on the other, so the nation is paralyzed by being assigned a future that never arrives. That's what we've got going on now in the city: these chain stores coming in, with the developers paying off city officials and downloading a future that freezes us in a monoculture. Yeah, call us and we'll rock for the Pyramid.

—Rev

Reverend,

Mine is an unholy confession: I am in love with my Swiffer. The smell of the chemical disinfectant-impregnated disposable mop pads, the 360-degree rotating handle, the devil-may-care disposability of it all . . . Reverend, help me! Save my soul!

—Dirty Girl, Baltimore, MD

Oh Dirty,

Oh, I know it, I know it. I've had an erotic thing for the disinfectant in really cheap motel rooms. I'm sitting here in the bus and I've copped somebody's wi-fi signal, I think from this motel the bus is parked next to. Yeah, I think I'm pulling the wi-fi right out of those disinfectant-laced carcinogenic rooms. My dirty little secret—and preachers have so many of them—is that I want to check into that place right now. Let's work through our sins, sister. It's how we learn.

—Rev

Hey Rev,

How often do you cleanse yourself of your shopping sins?
Of your commercial website where you can click and buy
the audio of Reverend Billy off eBay? Buy nothing day . . .
babies and devils . . . buy a ticket sliding scale 10–10,000
dollars. This is bullshit. This is a commercial enterprise.
Rev. Billy where is your Tammy Faye Baker? Your
evangelistic hypocrisy is gross. What do you have to say
for yourself when you say, "Don't buy their stuff buy my
stuff?" Congratulations, you went to jail and bragged
about how it boosted your publicity. How Honorable of
you. You're just as slick and sick as Starbucks. You use the
same victims. Shame on you. Try going back to why you
started. Were you charging for CDs then? Did you ask
10–10,000 dollars then? When did the evil commercial
virus infect you? Put that mirror up and see what you can
see.

—Suzanne

Dear Suzanne,

Good morning. Well, of course you're raising questions
that we discuss at our Stop Shopping group. For years we
were a neighborhood political group, doing fundraisers for
the greengrocer's union or painting out billboards of
offending transnationals. As we became better known (we

are celebrating our tenth anniversary) we were faced with a whole set of questions that we didn't have when I was alone sidewalk preaching. We're commercial in form sometimes, but it's easy to see that we are not industrial celebrities. Spreading an anticommercial message via some of the commercial system's own strategies and avenues is something that we have accepted and will continue to explore. We are making a movie now, but will always use whatever notoriety we achieve to help local activists. The media is one way that we make public statements in this day and age. We'll start with our friends at grassroots radio and Indy Media Centers, but today I'll be preaching on drive-time Denver radio, shouting into a cell phone by the side of the turnpike in Pennsylvania. I'll be shouting Stop Shopping, and the choir will be harmonizing, making music of our message. And maybe we will be heard.

—Reverend

Dear Rev,
I just read an article about your organization and your characterization of "MM" as the anti-Christ. I have been calling him the "Evil Mouse" for quite some time and would never buy anything from "Disney." I also belong to Adbusters and observe Buy Nothing Day. Every year when

I put up a new calendar I write BND in the appropriate day. I applaud you and wish you success in getting through to the mindless consumers.

—Greg

Greg,

Good to hear from a fellow congregant in this Resistance To Consumerism. I'm writing from Snowshoe, Pennsylvania. The choir and I just exorcized the local Post Office of its junk mail and the Post-mistress, Sophie, was so happy she started crying. She said, "Nobody ever cared! They don't even let us call it junk mail! We have to call it 'Business Bulk.'"

Tonight in Oberlin, Ohio, I'd like to preach about the surprise that exists in a good gift. We're busing through miles of tinsel and neon Santas. Are all these consumers really excited when they go into these Big Boxes and buy what everyone else is also buying?

At Christmas, the best gift has the joy of surprise. A good gift also confirms the relationship of the giver and the givee, which is ongoing. So surprise and tradition, seemingly opposites, go hand in hand with a good gift. Example: I may give you a print by Ansel Adams because of the way that I saw you pause before a mountain, but you didn't necessarily see me watching you. The satisfaction of the gift is that I surprised you by the thoroughness of my witness, I KNOW you, and the gift confirmed our relationship in a surprising way.

—Rev

Dear Rev,
Every so often I feel like giving into the b*llsh*t and wandering into the Church of Lard that is McDonald's to devour their babydrugfood in order to alleviate my product/consumer depression. Now, however, with the spirit of the Church Of StopShop inspiring me I now stand before the House of Ronald and just say no to their bogus delicrap, buns of air&sadanimal and creamy bins of plastic iced margarine. Thank you Reverand!

—Dr. Zoinks, London, England

Dear Dr. Zoinks,
Because I'm an indigo baby, part autistic and part the Archbishop of Canterbury, I had a "learning nightmare" long ago, during my babyhood, that I must share with you, Dr. Zoinks. First, I crawled up into my crib and waited there. Then my clown interns waggled three blobs over my face. They were like Calder mobiles from a sewage treatment plant in Queens. Hanging over me were

a blob of sugar, a blob of grease, and a blob of salt and I was starved into comic submission with Ronald's simple smile. The interns wore Ronald masks—a high-risk childhood trauma. I recoiled into a crib-death from which there was only one escape: the "learning nightmare" of unconditional resurrection. I woke up and the room was empty. My Life would now begin.

Oh, the bus is pulling over, where are we—ah, it's not a place it's an Exit.

—Rev

Dear Rev,

Amen. Although I am a Hindu, nothing ticks me off more than living in the Bible Belt where people praise Christ day-in and day-out, and as Christmas approaches many of these people I speak of go into hock, load up on debt on credit cards, all to buy presents.

Right now I'm somewhat "tight" financially but I do intend to send a donation to your noble cause to save American humanity in the future. You need to contact Jimmy Carter. You're both on the same page with this issue.

Sincerely,
Shakti

Dear Shakti,

Thank you so much for your kind letter. We do feel so strange sometimes, trying to stop the thing that everybody's doing. Christmas. Unbelievable. Yes what if we simply praised the birth of the baby who grew up to be the Prince of Peace. There's another supermall in the bus window. The malls all seem to be linking up—with no pause in between—out here. Highway 80. All the behemoths fuming and blurring. The choir is singing again, got the trumpet out and the electric piano out. We keep each other going. I can't stay depressed very long if I join in and sing for a while. That helps. Just stick with the praise and that's a lot of giving right there. Thanks Shakti. Merry Christmas!

—Rev

Posted on Revbilly.com December 18:

—might not answer confessions for a while—we were hit by a truck the night of dec 17, east of bryan, ohio—15 of us pulled from wreckage and—what a scene helicopters coming down onto the highway—taken to er's and trauma centers around northwestern ohio, mostly Toledo. Everybodys alive. We're at an econo-lodge on highway 80.

—rev

next morning—some of us who were unconscious have recovered completely and then there were heroes who were having everyone get treatment first and they turned out to have internal injuries—the director of our movie rob vanalkamade his ribs broke and stabbed his insides and we visited him yesterday—he's in terrible pain now—laid out white as a sheet—

next afternoon—bus is totaled—talking to tv crews who come to the econo lodge and meet us in the lobby—I'm here now after another media van goes—in the questions they get to the place where the conversation turns from injuries to "so what is this church? You want people to stop shopping?" "Yes we are on a mission to save Christmas from the shopocalypse."— we're watching news anchors struggling over the word 'shopocalypse' then one weatherman says "it's simple, *shopping* plus *apocalypse*—PUT THEM TOGETHER"—the weatherman knows which way the wind blows—

Tonight the choir sang a gospel song they invented called WE WILL LOSE OUR FEAR OF DRIVING—it looks like— well we have ten people back from observation—we've decided the tour will go on—savitri is staring at figures and on the phone—leasing a new bus—not bio-diesel though which is a drag—most of us out of the hospitals now—locals bringing us food here where we are stranded in the econo lodge

We're out in this subzero wasteland with the twisted metal of sammy the bus—dead in back of the truckstop across the frontage road, we go over and pray to the "fabulous unknown" thanking our companion force for the good luck that no-one died.

Sitting here, watching these folks hugging and walking around slowly, repairing spirits—I feel like the hope that consumption can be confronted in this joyous way, our idea, crossing the country to slow down shopping in America—I suddenly am aware of how we're not safe out here, opposing consumerism is close to opposing racism or homophobia out here in this huge wacky country—this is a strategy of educating often unwilling Americans and the whole thing carries terrible risks—we've still got five people in bed here in pain, having trouble breathing, looking into the faces of nurses and doctors—out here in this flat country covered with ice and long lines of 80 mile an hour trucks—the outer space of consumerism—

Local Quakers and peace-people offering their homes, bringing food to our doors—I just tear up when I see them—they have this look of knowledge about what we're doing—70 year olds living out here who worked to ban the bomb and got on the buses in freedom summer—I think a lot of us could get the idea from the bush and cheney presidency that out in America the peace had died away—that's not true at all—and I see 10,000 hits at the website just today, hello everyone we're OK, savitri is laughing through the thin motel walls, laughing with friends—but I might not try to pastor too much on the confessions for a few days—got to concentrate here on the immediate, the present, and the simple things—

Post to Revbilly.com, Dec 20:
I will not forget this. We walked into the Mall of America with 60 Minnesotans in extra choir robes. Just as we had hoped, the people in the Mall thought we were a choir hired for Christmas festivities and just as we hoped the MOA main stage was empty and waiting for us and STOP SHOPPING rang out and—wonderful

Then we marched through the place—7 football fields of selling and so many tons of Christmas tinsel and plastic santas and standing amidst it all the lightly-dulled consumers, caught in the early stages of a dream they haven't plumbed—and don't let me talk down to anybody here JUST BECAUSE I'M SHOUTING STOP SHOPPING DOESN'T MEAN I'M RES-URRECTED FROM IT—

We ended up in abercrombie and fitch underneath a big stuffed moosehead, hanging his head over the cash register, while hundreds of us are on our knees to this great dead moose-face, with the snoopy ferris wheel spinning in the background and a dozen police persons clucking PRIVATE PROPERTY PRIVATE PROPERTY but we're just caroling sir! It's Christmas! We're caroling! You don't like sweatshops do you? Do you think this is right?

Dear Rev. Billy,

I fear I may be committing the greatest of evils almost everyday. You see sir, I am a "Graphic Designer." While I aspire to do good in this world—design a better way/finding/signage system for NYC's underground, for example—mostly what I do is design advertising . . . or closely related materials. I make my living by creating seductive images that induce people to purchase things they don't really need. I've tried to work for things I "believed" in, art galleries and museums . . . but quickly realized that even there in these sacred places ALL was commodity. Dear sir, what can I do? Are all images evil in the end? Is mine a purely evil profession? Do I need to look into a career change? Can I and my many colleagues, who are also my friends, be saved?

Yours in Hope, HG, Christ Church (sic), New Zealand

Dear HG:

Out here on the highway (somewhere in Iowa now) there is so much advertising that it's easy to say: YES IT'S ALL EVIL! GET OUT OF THAT BUSINESS. But something about your address—Christ Church, New Zealand—I'm thinking, Oh—maybe it's not so bad where you are.

When it becomes necessary to commit to a day-job that is Evil, then in your spare time you can "subvert the day-job." Yes, let's not pretend. Advertising is killing us. Why can't

Americans adequately wake up to the war? Or to global warming? Why are we consenting to this society-wide hypnosis—letting our communities become stupid pavement horizons? We are dumbfounded by ads. Thousands every day. WHO HERE IS NOT SICK TO DEATH OF GOOD GRAPHICS?

So please, subvert your day-job. Work to undo the damage you inflict by means of an after-hours stealthy nighttime counter-intelligence. I met some dynamic folks who work in ad agencies. They have formed an astonishing group called DYKE ACTION MACHINE and at night they turn the tables on their own day. These women literally reverse the power of ads with their street theater. At DykeActionMachine.com you will see "The agit-prop group armed with wheatpaste, ire, and WILD GRAPHIC TALENTS."

—Rev

Dear Rev. Billy:
I own and drive a $100,000 Mercedes S-Class nearly 100 miles a day to and from [my] downtown office, frequently driving down HOV lanes. I entertain several people a day at very expensive restaurants, where the $500+ bill is paid by my company that will often make 100 fold in return for the bit of schmoozing I do. At the end of the year, I'll get a $400K bonus on top of my almost one million dollar yearly salary. On the weekends, I will hang out in the

Hamptons or take the yacht out. Sometimes, I will arrange for a little "out of town meeting," and get some corporate jet time on a Cessna Citation X and cruise at mach 0.92 at five miles up and head to Vegas, where I will do some minor schmoozing and blow maybe $40 Big G's at the tables. To make myself feel better, I'll then go and buy something really big and expensive, like a new $25,000 entertainment system. I won't give a dime to charity and laugh at the suckers that have to take mass transit and suckers like you that only wish you could be where I am. I *am* the consumer devil and I will lure all your dear little ones with the intoxicating dreams to be me once they wake up from their delusional loser liberal, wussy, pansy-ass hissy fits and realize they're 30 and still losers and way way behind in the rat race. Muhahahahaha. . . . Come to me O, dear sweet child of mine and suckle on the sweet nectar of gluttonous greed and intoxicating self-indulgence.

—Karl, Greenwich, CT

Karl,
Is all this only a pose? I mean, it's very funny, your letter—but you sound as if even you do not find your Life that interesting.

—Rev

Reverend,

Hi. My name is Carol Ann. I'm a recovering Shopaholic. I used to shop as a bonding activity with my mother and sister. Sort of like the boys going fishing. Also loved to buy things online. Then came the Credit Card Apocalypse. I had to hit bottom to realize my problem. Now I'm shopping-free! I no longer even like the smell of shopping! I realize that my shopping was only fueling our corporate-owned government. Right on, Rev. Billy. Keep preaching the word. You are one talented brother.

—Carol Ann, Spring, TX

Dear Carol Ann,

Thanks for your letter. We are rumbling along toward Lawrence, Kansas. I notice something in your note—that moment that slips by—the step from shopping with your mom and sister to shopping in young adulthood, ready to start your own family. When we cross that bridge, after leaving mom and dad, sometimes we are vulnerable. For a couple years we are undefended. The marketers then rush in with their actors and models who say, "Bond with me . . . Keep spending . . . I'm your new family . . ." I guess the most famous example is the Plastic Avalanche in college—you can get a half dozen credit cards before you turn twenty.

The Devil studies our love. Knowing how we bond, the Devil researches it still further, in all its forms, in our families, with lovers and friends, with members of the community. They will mimic our bonding perfectly, and the actors and models begin their sell sell sell Death march. Here they come. They have fire in their eyes. They're getting closer and closer! No! MOTHER FATHER GOD SAVE US FROM THESE ARMIES OF FAKE FAMILY!

The buses are pulling into lovely downtown Lawrence, lots of independent shops surviving on the main street here . . .

—Reverend

I ate at McDonald's today, and I feel terrible, what can I do?

—Michael, Victoria, Canada

Pick up some trash!

—rev

Rev Billy,

I get this urge to buy comfortable cotton clothes even though I already have lots of comfortable cotton clothes, I think the variety will make my Life more interesting or more yummy or something. It's like wanting to buy several gallons of milk. Sure, you know you will use it all eventually—but when does eventually come?????

—Basema, Brooklyn, NY

Dear Basema,

You have here a series of soft-focus desires: "more interesting," and "yummy," and "comfortable." But really they are blurs inside a larger desire, which is "I get this urge." Now, let's go all the way to your final words, "when does 'eventually' come?" "Eventually" does not serve us, Sister Basema. It only puts off direct action.

My suggestion is: Take twelve pages and write the name of a month across each page. Then write down what you'll need over those four seasons—no vague words like "more interesting," and "eventually." Straightforwardly, what do you really need? If you separate yourself from what you own, it can be almost like asking, "Who am I? Who am I really?"

And then there's the question "Where am I?" Which keeps coming up while traveling across America, in this sea of identical details. The same dozen logos wherever we go. Toto, looking out of this bus window, I don't think we're in Kansas anymore, but how would we know?

—Rev

Dear Reverend Billy,

I wear Nikes. I know it's wrong, I really do. But what else can I do? I'm a member of the nightlife industry and trend is a necessary evil. I need counsel now more than ever. Can you help me? Tragically hip in Hell's Kitchen.

—Justin, NY, NY

Brother Justin,

Well a trend doesn't start with a thousand people out of the blue wearing a swoosh on their feet. There is always a friend who steps out with a new color, a new flip of fabric, cut of hair, a phrase with a new shout in it. Suddenly— mysteriously—what was just fun with friends becomes something an increasing number of people do, sparks a trend . . . that's why those cool hunters spy on the high schools in the Bronx. Nike is studying the kids to feed to them for a price what the kids themselves invented. Oh, sometimes the sinful chutzpah leaves me in the Lake of Hellfire.

But Nike doesn't want to get REALLY hip, they don't want to meet one of these kids who's handing out information at school about Nike sweatshops in Viet Nam. I'm the cool hunter looking for THAT trend. Brother Justin, be truly hip: Take the nightlife industry down a new path. You're already hip—just create now. Move forward on your own! Make the road by walking!

—Rev

Dear Reverend Billy,

I wish I had enough money to NOT shop at Wal-Mart because it is the Devil. Poor people must shop there because of the low prices and therefore Wal-Mart can keep its employed poor and the cycle continues. I will try my hardest to shop at my local store. I guess all I can do is just give my problem up to the "God of the Living Wage."

—Robert, St. Petersburg, FL

Brother Rob,

I'm answering your letter just after "Whirling" in a Wal-Mart in Omaha. In a Whirl you go up and down the aisles pushing an empty shopping cart, in a long line that turns and turns and goes straight and turns again, through the Big Box, for an hour. You never put anything into the cart and keep pushing, looking straight ahead. If anyone stops you and demands an exclamation, just say "I'm not shopping." And now, back in the bus, we are high from this. We are absolutely flying. You see, something happens at the forty-minute point, the zen trance kicks in, then all the cartoons and celebrity shills on the bottles and packages seem to come to life! It's like you've been in one of those sense-deprivation tanks. The smells get really harsh, crossing from the bar-b-que section into women's lingerie is like falling through space—and the colors are so strong they leave trails in your eyes like camera-flashes.

Anyway, about Wal-Mart: Its breakthrough was that with its size it could depress local wages to the point where its discounts became the only option for its victimized customers. The plea that "the poor have no option" can't be true forever, though, because who among us red-blooded Americans will allow this con-job to continue? Are we resigning ourselves to this colonization? No, we're not. This isn't the future that we dream of. This is not what we will hand over to our children. Wal-Mart will not be reformed. Either it will be unionized all the way from its sweatshops to its Big Boxes or it will be broken into small parts.

Another thing: The discounts at Wal-Mart are a myth. Studies show that they discount the most obvious items at the head of the aisle. Wal-Mart has discovered that we consumers cannot remember the prices for most items, but we depend on things like toilet paper, soap, cereal, garbage bags to indicate to us a price level. Walk a few paces past these staples, move up the aisle a bit, and Wal-Mart is adding dollars to the cost.

Of course, if Wal-Mart has a competing store that is still alive in the neighborhood, they'll keep their prices radically low until the other store is shuttered. For many years that kind of price-gouging was not legal in the United States, but the retailers wore down Congress and got their way. Now the small Indy stores are sitting ducks. WAL-MART IS THE DEVIL!

—Rev

Posted to Revbilly.com blog, Dec 20:
Savitri takes the bus microphone: "There's this cemetery just behind the Wal-Mart world headquarters. We'll start there." And soon we're blearily, fully clothed, propelled into our morning by the dead ancestors and retail Devils.

We gathered our choir from the homes of the amazing Eureka Springs church volunteers, who last night took us from our bus stumbling with fatigue and led us to their beds and roused us at 5 am and fed us—and now off to Savitri's dead, to haunt the cemetery behind Wal-Mart, in our ethereal white robes.

Singing the bit of life that clung to the front of the tomb-stones, the names—singing the names—and the date of birth—singing the birthdays—and the date of passing—singing the names and births and Deaths and trying to feel the Life in the resting dead under the frozen lawns of this cemetery, right behind the barbed wire fence behind the Wal-Mart control center, where the happy face execs were just now parking and slowly walking toward their offices. I suppose we slowed them down even more.

We prayed and sang and marched. From the dead we walked in a long line, putting hands on the singer in front, and now accompanied by corporate cops in SUVs, talking on cellphones, big obese cops. I tried to preach, continuing with the power of the lives from the cemetery. "We have millions of Americans in our bodies, the cheated and the robbed, there is a time for anger, let's go to the high altar of the Shopoca-lypse!" and we face the front of the place finally, but the place had no front. There was a fairly modest sign out front, and we faced it, but it had no power. It said HOME OFFICE and we prayed and cursed at it and there was nothing pressing back against us.

The front door behind the sign had the anonymous style of a brick building behind the gymnasium of a state college. There was no here, here. We couldn't find a personality. No culture at the center. We gyrated and jumped, danced and sang. I was upset, shaking. We had filled with the lives of Americans whose American dreams were economically killed and filled our spirits with the children working in the sweat-shops and now, having taken on this weight, we couldn't find the front door of the Devil's house. So then I decided it was time for the reverend to show some leadership. I dove into a shrub—not the grandest nor most effective gesture in my years of ministering, I will admit.

We're on the bus now going south. Tricked by the Devil, unable to confront him when we wanted to. Bummed out.

Reverend,

I would like to share my experience as a low level employee in corporate America. After working as an auto mechanic for many years at independent repair shops, I decided I needed a break from the stress of dealing honestly and faithfully with a consumer base that has had its confidence shaken by today's service industry ("my water pump was fine before you fixed the brakes!"). Figuring, naively, that working at a parts store would be a nice easy steady change of pace to relax into for a few years, I was hired by O'Rielly auto parts (a company I found later to have contributed to the Death of possibly as many small businesses as the evil Wally) as a counter man. After only a week or so of employment I noticed that around the back area of the store, hidden from customers, were a total of fifteen posters threatening dire happenings towards employee theft. This started me thinking of the phrase, "People live up to the expectations others have of them." As a result, the posters seemed counterproductive.

I knew then that there must be another reason for them, that being instilling fear and guilt into employees where none was seemingly needed. The need for the negative reinforcement seemed to me to stem from a realization at the corporate level that any employee they hire will likely be below the minimum standard that a knowledgeable auto parts customer, or a harried store manager, would expect. Further this was proven by the ignorance of basic auto repair by most of my fellow employees, even those in critical jobs like district managers and warehouse personnel. Some employees showed a contempt for customers with their genuine, and sometimes critical, need for the correct part for a car that may be the only one they can afford to get them to work and back safely. After gamely working at this job for over a year, I began to ask too many questions, and became irate with fellow workers over the shabby treatment that customers received.

—Bill, Bakersfield, CA

Brother Bill!
I'm reading your letter somewhere in suburban Dallas, at an I-net café. I'm so grateful for it. Since Bentonville I've lost my way, lost. The dignity of honest work—and the solidarity among workers—where do we start this

reformation? If the place to start change is with a fellow citizen, who wants the "right part"? Just be of service. You have revived me, Bill!

—The Rev

Hello Reverend Billy,

I am doing research on your organization and just had one question for you: I was wondering how did you get started with this idea of stop shopping and why? Thank you so much for your time and insight.

—Noy

Dear Noy,

Today we preached and sang from a flatbed truck up and down the strip in Las Vegas. Oh, we have our mojo back! Caesar's Palaces and Eiffel Towers looming up into the night sky and exhausted-looking Christmas consumers below. For hours and hours we would sneak up on people with our surprise Stop Shopping anthems. This is a dirty neon Babylon and I'm slumped over the email congregation now and I get your letter. Are you a student? Or an intern from a magazine?

Look. It's an emergency. Vegas makes me realize how we've invented our own Nuremberg super-rally.

Consumerism has us facing one way—toward the product. We're in formation. Our gestures, our memories, and our senses are all organized toward the point of purchase. All day long, they have got people yearning forward, marching toward a completion of the consumption event. We are walking through a tube toward a light. Occasionally something breaks through our hypnosis, there may be a flicker of light on the wall of the tube. Oil wars, extinction spikes, freak storms, darkened main streets—we can't quite register that they have taken place. We sense that something is going wrong, but we are told that the solution to any problems is to buy more. Even Democracy, Independence, Love—our grandest ideas of ourselves—are now products, so we keep moving through the tube.

Well, Noy, how did we "start with this idea"? When you want to save your Life, your imagination is ready.

—Rev

Dear Rev. Billy,
Last month I had to accompany my partner into a Target to help her buy a tricycle for her grandson. In order to maintain my sensibilities I decided to selflessly hawk the products on sale there, with the chant, "Get your Chinese slave labor products here! Our slave labor products are

CHEAPER than the other slave labor products at ALL the other mega-conglomerate stores! Get it now before they try to unionize! Thank You!" Needless to say no one responded, but I felt better for screaming the TRUTH. Somehow I wonder if I managed to spread any Christmas Jeer. Dear Rev. Billy, am I absolved?

Your Faithful Deacon,

Shanti, Cambridge, MA

Dear Sister Shanti:

Sounds like you had a good time! Yes, you are absolved— can I get off the hook, too? Interesting question: What is it about shouting in retail space? Where does the intense fear of doing it—and then the undeniable pleasure from finally letting out the STOP SHOPPING!!—come from? Maybe the fact that a communication that doesn't originate from products is in the air?

Yes, we did almost exactly the same thing as you— yesterday at the Victoria's Secret in Flagstaff, Arizona. We got off the bus and each of us in the church had to choose our script: Do I shout about the sweatshops as I hold the high style thongs and teddys up in the fluorescent air? Or do I shout about the Supermodels of the Shopocalypse clear-cutting trees for their million-catalogs-a-day drug habit? It can be very artless. Just shout the information near the point of purchase until the security marches toward you yelling "Private Property! Private Property!" Then switch to a whisper and get confidential promises from the rent-a-cops that they as individuals don't approve of the sweatshops and the contribution of crotchless undies to global warming. Amen.

—Rev

Dear Reverend Billy,

I saw your confessional booth yesterday in Santa Monica, but missed my chance to confess in person. I sin regularly by shopping at The Home Depot. There are no more local hardware stores left in my area—only chain stores. The Home Depot is terrible—no service at all, poor products, untrained staff (if you can find one). But: the cheapest prices in town. I am working on my own house to save money. Every time I send The Home Depot an excoriating letter describing my unsatisfying experience at their store, The Home Depot responds by sending me a $10 gift card. They also send a self-effacing email. Then, I have a $10 gift card that I feel compelled to spend by visiting and shopping at The Home Depot. How can I get out of this vicious cycle? Plus, what do we do when there are no longer locally owned hardware stores in a given region, and shoppers are forced to choose between giant chains for their hardware purchases. Merry Christmas.

—Sus, Marina, CA

Dear Sus,

First remember that our "no-choice" predicament is a trap set by the chain stores. Starbucks is notorious for this—clustering in a neighborhood, killing the locals by picking off every possible customer wandering in the area. And of course, Starbucks can afford to open coffee shops whose only purpose is to pick off these strays, starve out the independent diners and cafes, then close when everybody's gone. We are left, finally, with no choice. This scenario has played out again and again across the country with corrupted officials looking the other way.

Second—and this one is our own sin—we end up shopping in chains and Big Boxes, giving up and giving in, when we are IN A HURRY. So often the item we seek IS available, but would take some time to find it. But listen: Local economies are starting up all over the world. People are saying—"I have this, do you have that? Let's trade." There is a very important movement springing up around food issues. Go to Locavores.com and Buylocalfood.com to get some facts. These folks are CELEBRATING THE LOCAL FOODSHED! Sus, a new economy can start modestly. Look for your item in a neighbor's garage (after asking for permission first!), in a local used-stuff sheet, or ask for what you need with a sign on the grocery store bulletin board. Start up the new old tradition. What a gift!

One final note: Ace Hardware is a locally owned cooperative. It is not a Lowe's or a Home Depot. Let's not confuse our angels and demons.

—Rev

Hi there Rev,

Just read about you in the Paul Kingsnorth book "One No, Many Yeses." I too am really fucked off with the big corporate takeover sucking the character out of society. I will be flyposting the Tesco stores in my area, but how can we see the return of small local business, when all people seem to want is convenience? I thought about organizing a boycott of a single store . . . not for a day but for a year. This should cripple the store and force it to close down . . . I think. What do you think?

Be great to hear from you, I'll spread the word about your good work.

Take it easy,

Alfonso

Brother,

On the far end of things, we human beings will join with the wind, water, and air to stop the Big Boxes. They can't survive because their fossil-fuel based economy will kill us all and our species has the will to survive. And what about our direct action today and tomorrow? Yikes, there's Los Angeles. There it is down in that haze.

Where was I? Today we're going into six supermalls in LA to sing and preach and hand out information. We've got a new idea we're gonna try: wading out into traffic jams and foisting our Fabulous Worship on the congregation of motorists!

(two days later . . .)

Dear Alfonso,

Looks like I didn't send that letter, or something happened, Los Angeles happened, in mid-thought. I'll admit, though, that sometimes I despair of small moves and I want that grand revolution from the history books to come back with all the drama. CHANGE-A-LUJAH! I just spent some time in the Disneyland jail, hoping something I did would change things. I don't know—there's no way of knowing whether I'm effecting a change in this famous sweatshop company with the smiling rat logo. We sang and preached to people in Main

Street USA, interrupted their act of faith, their Disney moment. LET'S TAKE OUR MAGIC BACK HOME! It sounds like you might find yourself, Alfonso, stymied in the way even the most gung-ho of us are, once in a while. We're kyboshed by the difficulty of imagining our penetration of Consumerism's New World Order, where a couple dozen companies surround us every waking moment with their logos. (And consumers look at us like we're crazy if we raise our voices a little bit.)

(next day again . . .)

Flying over the USA now, crossing the Mississippi, the trail of tears in reverse, up 40,000 feet. Our Shopocalypse Tour over, and did we stop the shopping down there?

Alfonso it IS imposing, but revolutions don't begin at the end, and they don't begin at the beginning either. They begin in several places at different times, with the armies of compassion rising from the past with so many anonymous martyrs. When we are given that dramatic critical mass that everyone talks about for many years into the future—when Rosa Parks finds her bus seat, or Mario Savio jumps up on his police car, or Cleve Jones picks up the old blanket for his AIDS quilt, or Lech Walesa stands on a barrel in his shipyard, or Wanghari Maathi dreams of her forest in Kenya—those burning tipping points come as a gift from so many places and so many people and suddenly—a mystery of creation—the moment that changes us is unmistakable.

Can we plan a revolution? Partly yes and partly no. There had to be lots of parallel failed strategies for the one brave moment to break through the cultural inertia. I know we'll live and die trying. I look down at America from this jet—and what a mad riddle it is!

LETTER FROM DISNEYLAND JAIL, DECEMBER 25, 2005

OK I'm in jail, no doubt about that. The Anaheim city prison, on Christmas night. This afternoon, at 1 p.m., we jumped into the Disney 50th Anniversary Christmas Day parade on Main Street USA in front of Mickey and Snow White and Goofy and performed our church-work for—

thirty minutes?—until finally I got pushed through a seam in the wall.

This jailer here is pacing and humming along with the song White Christmas, which is broadcast from his blaster, on the floor out of view to the left of my bars, about fifty feet away. This is a small cell, maybe four feet by seven feet, but I'm glad I'm not in a group tank. This is definitely a California jail—it's all painted white, even the bars. My White Christmas.

I've been trying to lie down. The single bench, a concrete ledge on the narrow end away from the door, is too short to curl up, or brace my legs up on the wall. I finally fold my legs up into my t-shirt and let the fabric hold me in a ball, then pull my preacher coat over that. Then I go into the on-purpose sleep of incarceration, a yoga practiced over the course of my 50 lock-ups. My self-hypnosis is supposed to change doing time to doing dreams. I try to picture what we did today, with the Magic Castle in the background, all the thousands of families . . .

The jailer is not happy—not happy at all—to be here with the holiday drunks, still caroling sloppily, and this ridiculous Elvis impersonator in the priest's collar. (I always leave it on in jail because it's safer that way.) The jailer acts like a tough guy, and he's angry to be here working on Christmas night—striding over to shout at some Mexican kid. Did the ex-CIA guys who work for Disney design this torture for us in Bing Sing? Will I emerge tomorrow morning with *an insatiable need to shop?*

The nice cop at Personal Effects, where I manila-enveloped my belt and wallet, let me keep my old piebald composition book and a pen. So, unable to concentrate on my reverie through Bing the Jailer's attack muzak, I'm writing now—but slowly. Mostly, I'm sitting here like a frozen frontyard Reverend Billy, nearly paralyzed by the jail-house White Christmas—the transmitted distillation of the thousands of snowy reindeer songs on the sound systems in our 5,000 miles of supermalls. It makes me want to write my way out of jail.

Twenty-four hours ago we saw the green interstate sign for DISNEYLAND. We felt the mad magic right away. Where was the falsetto laughter of Mickey Mouse coming from? The unappeased souls of the Disneyland dead? Now, an interstate off-ramp isn't where you expect to have any sensation at all, unless the landscape offers you a car accident. But Mickey Mouse gives you the creeps in the blandest places. A frisson of fear came up our legs, the whole choir went from singing to silence as we turned and lost altitude. We crowded into an Econo-Lodge up 405 toward Los Angeles, but just inside Anaheim's city limits, and therefore inside this Vatican City run by Goofy and

1,200 underunemployed method actors and Walt's frozen comic brush.

In the Econo-Lodge, the concierge had Mickey's eyes and Mickey's ears and we were afraid—the anthropomorphized rodent logo was blended into everything we touched. Anaheim is not just a company town. It's a step past that. It is Mickey's bulbous face bubbling up through the sticky polymers of every surface. The bedsheets that feel like massive plastic place mats have Mickey's beaming head in the quilted flowers. The coffee machine in the lobby sounds like Donald quacking. There seem to be men in sunglasses in the parking lot moving slowly between unmarked cars. Can we say "THEY KNOW WE ARE HERE?"

We knew that our Disneyland invasion, scheduled for the next day, needed a thorough strategy session that could not be anywhere near a surveillance camera. Savitri assembled all forty of us in a single motel room. Each group, divided into units of six or eight, would infiltrate the theme park the following morning in shifts, entering at the top of each hour. The groups would go to separate designated "lands"—Frontierland for shoot-outs and pow-wows, or Californialand for a simulation of . . . what you just drove out of, or Tikiland, for an oriental jumble of the entire southern hemisphere. By noon we would all be inside, Savitri and I coming last, for the action itself.

The altos and basses would get into their robes in the Tiki Room bathroom and the sopranos and tenors would do the same in the Tomorrowland stalls. The two lines of singers should be walking in step midway between the two bathrooms, in the center of Main Street USA, at 1:10 PM. I would join from the side, where I would then peel out of the Ali G black track suit covering my white suit and priest's collar. Our cameramen would be positioned up and down Main Street, flipping their cassettes to runners, who would escape from the park every five minutes. In the sweltering one-person-per-square-foot motel room, there was a thorough recitation of the scheme by Savitri that was then recited back to Savitri by the leader of each commando group. We recited the plan until exhausted, and there was no oxygen left in the room, and then we sat there together, sweating. We prayed, "Oh Fabulous Unknown, do not abandon us as we pass into Logoland . . . "

After our prayer, we split up. What social groups formed, which individuals ended up together, was always fascinating for those among us who are social scientists and gossips. On the night before the mouse, some lived by the hard party. Others went off to be alone, reading, emailing. It was the night before a cultural invasion and you could almost hear a soundtrack from *Cape Fear* or *The Longest Day*. Out here in Interstateland you couldn't go for a walk, but you could grab the remote and check out the comedy of Orange County cable TV. Some outrageous preachers there, some Cuisinarts for sale that don't just cut your vegetables they listen to your problems and drive you to work. Then of course the aerobic yoga *Bay Watch*—like semi-porn on the beach—Hey! Let's be healthy the California way.

From the distance of New York, and during the tour across the country, the vaguely Bavarian "Magic Castle" with the two-legged animals in glowing tuxedos had always loomed on the western horizon. As we traveled closer, the upcoming invasion of Disneyland began to seem less funny and folkloric and more serious and strange. For one thing, there was the troubling atmosphere of suburban southern California, this White Christmas where I am now jailed. This is the land of Ronald Reagan and John Wayne—and is, along with Lynchburg, Virginia maybe, the cultural epicenter of America's apocalyptic endgame. This is a land of repeatedly announced values that, it turns out, cannot be experienced, because the land has been retailed and malled to make direct experience impossible. The physical world here only allows, what, shopping and surfing? The locals must shoot their moral fervor into action movies, Bush/Clinton/Reagan wars, immigrant vigilantism, apocalyptic Christianity . . .

Mickey has imagineered the imagination out of the air. Here off this off-ramp we felt Disneyland's sad power, how it was summoning forth the Shopocalypse.

This morning, Savitri and I, Fred Askew with his camera, and Katrina, our friend and native to these parts, drive into the parking lot within the parking lot within the parking lot. We cannot see the Magic Castle yet, or the famous concrete Matterhorn that looms over Main Street USA. It is unbelievable to us that every single Stop Shopping singer got in with the bright gospel red robe in their backpacks and purses. This makes us smile: a good omen. Disneyland is a designated terrorist target, they say. In the landmarks of Americana, it's up there with Lady Liberty and Mount Rushmore—according to the public servants at Homeland Security.

So, as we stand in the first of two lines—in the entrance rituals—the security folks search our suitcase perfunctorily. I feel the general BUY SOMETHING music rising from its source in a hundred feature films going back into the mists of pop time. A monorail train sails over the trees. Undeniably, there is excitement here. And the people!

The place is very crowded. So many families have decided to spend Christmas at Disneyland. One of the singers had said Disneyland used to be closed on sacred days. Of course, now The High Church Of Retail And

Used Magic has moved into all the holy days on the calendars. As the four of us move up in the second line, the music of Disneyland closes in around us, all Disney, oh yes, the great media corporation is stalking us. The company with the power to convene the US Congress and extend the copywritten Life of Mickey Mouse to eighty years . . . is singing to us. Someday My Prince Will Come, Elton John with his lions, Chim Chim Cheree, the theme from the Mouskateers, and what's this? Ragtime, Scott Joplin? Cementing it all, mysterious choirs invoking winter wonderland scenes for the thousands, fanning themselves with Mickey-shaped fans in their Bermuda shorts.

Then the ticket window shut in our face. A tired-looking lady is announcing that the park is closed! NO! Allen is immediately on the radio to James, the choir director—this cannot happen. We are all on airplanes tomorrow morning, back to our jobs in NY. Not to mention, if Reverend Billy is stuck at the gate, we're out the $2,000 for everyone else's $50-per-head ticket, and the tour's climax is gone. We could go back to the Econo-lodge and have romances and long talks . . . . Yes, we could make a French film. THIS IS CRAZY! The ticket lady says, "No, the park is over capacity. No one else is allowed in until later tonight."

This is a particularly vicious court injunction from Murphy's Law.

And the emotional conclusion, the arrival, the release and deliverance from malled America by way of the planned trial and public tribulation of Billy, suffering for our shopping sins. All the moral art of it, our year of hopes, up in smoke. Our Lewis-and-Clark expedition across the wilderness of America's shopping season . . . I began to lose it.

Savitri grabbed my arm. "You do not preach until you are on Main Street." I froze in my ridiculous Ali G tracksuit and pointy big-hair-hiding Dr. Seuss hat. Savitri and James were getting static on the radio phone. Then the nightmare deepened: Yes, it appeared that all radio and cell phone signals *are jammed in Disneyland*. But of course! We should have thought of that! We stood in the crowd, amazed, and sneaking glances at plainclothes Disney cops. Were they closing in?

"This cannot happen," said Savitri, through clenched teeth. She then walked over to the window and pounded on it with her fist. In polite, grinning Disneyland this is the kind of sound that stops everything around it. We froze. A hundred yards of small families froze. Here was our first small opposition to the mouse, and it sent ripples through the crowd, now stranded with nothing to do for

Christmas day. A hand pushed the small door back, and immediately Savitri sagged against the opening like Desdemona making her final gesture, prostrating before the god of tragedy. "WHAT AM I GOING TO DO? MY FRIENDS AND I HAVE PLANNED THIS TRIP FOR A YEAR? NO ONE TOLD US THIS COULD HAPPEN? NONE OF THE DISNEY PEOPLE I TALKED TO ON THE PHONE, NOBODY EVER SAID COME HERE EARLY IN THE DAY. NOW OUR FRIENDS ARE INSIDE AND WE'RE OUT HERE!" And then, to my surprise, she started sobbing.

The battered ticket-takers had all gone halfway back into their regular lives already, little coats half-off and dreaming of a cigarette break. But Savitri somehow managed to gather these exhausted ticket-people to the window in the wall, and in the gasping conversation we heard the words "exception" and then "emergency," and Allen and Katrina and I traded a small smile. Not that anyone in the long line behind us was really expecting to get in, but this forlorn crowd of our-day-off families was getting some entertainment, anyway, in this desperate form. Then Savitri took the wad of bills she was carrying for the choir's $20-a-day allowance, and added that to her histrionics, waving it in her fist. As she pressed for her emergency exception, her screams and sobbings alternated with soothing sounds and lawsuit threats. Now the window opened wider and our bills moved toward the opening.

The deal? It took the whole wad. How very Disney of you. The whole $500. Savitri had purchased two twelve-month Fiftieth Anniversary deluxe passes to all Disney parks in the known world, including Hong Kong and Paris. Yes we now had the crème-de-la-crème access—across the moat and into the land of singing logos. So, we were in. With our loss of all our remaining money, the eighty years of Disney music seemed to swell. Or was that just that our emergency had passed and we now could hear and see again? We had been swatted by Tinkerbell's magic wand.

As our butterflies subsided, our dreamstate unfolded. We were hyperaware that all the people of our Disneyland action—the singers, musicians, and lawyers—were all now out of touch. We would have to somehow find our church members in the vast, dreaming crowd. We were now walking slowly up the perfectly scrubbed late 1800s Midwestern Main Street USA with its slightly shrunk store-fronts. (I had read that this main street replica was reduced to 80 percent of its historical model.) We stood there and looked out over a sea of consumers, all with their backs turned to us, looking up into the sky.

This was the Fiftieth Anniversary of the founding of

Disneyland, and the crowd was all gazing up at the faux
Matterhorn, where near the top, an enormous Mickey
Mouse was mountain-climbing up a long series of large
numbers, with, you guessed it, 50 at the summit. Minnie
was scared, Mickey was stupid, and Donald Duck, a duck
far out of water, was urging Mickey to fall, quacking his
abusive jokes. Mickey would slip down, with Minnie and
40,000 kids screaming as he fell onto an unseen
mattress. Then the great mouse would todder back up
toward the big 5-0 once again before falling back again,
Minnie crying and Donald flapping his duck bill madly. I
was as consumerized as the next person, staring up with
my mouth slackly open. Savitri told me to warm up my
voice during the general sighs and screams of the crowd
below—and I did. When Minnie led the crowd below in
shouting, "WE LOVE YOU MICKEY!" And then
"CONGRATULATIONS ON YOUR 50TH MICKEY!" I
was trying my little grunts, shouts, letting out falsetto
whoops, I gradually got my voice louder and louder. Then
suddenly Savitri punched my shoulder. The concrete and
spackle mountain was still. Mickey and Minnie and
Donald had frozen. Loudspeakers on all sides were
making a breathy announcement, "If you would like to
take a picture of this historical moment, Mickey doesn't
want you to miss it, he'll wait for you to run to the camera

store on Main Street, right next to the piano player on the east side, you can buy a good camera full of film, go ahead, Mickey and Minnie will wait for you. You'll have this moment forever."

I had to sit down. Savitri and I watched the crowd get in line for history. And I began to have trouble with my voice. We knew we wouldn't get a bullhorn through security, so I would have to get my own body's bellows vibrating nice and loud. But I had never felt this way before. I was frightened, disoriented, and my throat felt like metal. Savitri began to talk to me like a boxing coach. "Eat something. Some protein. Keep breathing." And so I sat there with a $12 Mickey-shaped bowl full of chili, and my Mickey-shaped toast, and let out occasional groans and vowel scales and big sighs to loosen my voice, as the crowd in Main Street shouted "GO FOR IT MICKEY! GO TO THE TOP! FIFTY YEARS IS SURE A LOT!" and the army of brand new cardboard cameras flashed to document this moment, a new height for western civilization.

Then it was one o'clock. I was looking at the Mickey Mouse at the top of the Magic Matterhorn and wondering about the nonunion actor who was looking out across this great plain of consumers, peering through the little mesh window in Mickey's mouth. He's feeling the drop-off of

the cliff below him, I'll bet, but he probably has that
mountaineering belt around his waist and someone
talking to him in his ear bud. He probably wants to check
the belt, make sure it's all there, but his hands are deep
inside his colossal three-fingered mits. He's waving them
to the beat of "the Circle of Life," sawing the air out over
the yawning abyss of Christmas consumption, while above
him the ears loom like floppy radar dishes. "It's one o-
clock. Are you ready?" Savitri said, from her Mickey-
shaped chair. We are really caught inside the logo of
Mickey's face here aren't we? We're inside the most
famous logo in the world. Logoland. I feel this vertigo. I
have to use the bathroom. "Make it quick." OK. I look for
a can, and as I go, I'm watching that actor up there on the
tip of the anniversary summit, and I'm thinking that he
REALLY invaded the logo.

On my way to the loo, the bazaar of rabid buying
pushes me against the wall, and the wall is varnished
bamboo with an eave of trinkets and feathers—it's
Rudyard Kipling's Jungle Boy land—with a soundtrack of
screaming birds over a disco backbeat. The birds are still
singing in the bathroom. In there, all these men are
standing around, doing nothing, blinking their eyes.
There was nothing untoward about it. Some of them were
fathers, and they had their sons wait with them, too. I

couldn't figure it out. I asked them, "What's wrong?" and they just mumbled that they were taking a break. Oh, I see, it's an actual *restroom* then. They were taking a psychic respite from the Magic Kingdom's onslaught.

While in the stall, I was aiming my ass out of my layers of the Ali G tracksuit and the Reverend's full chicken and suddenly I dropped one of my body-mikes into the Mickey-shaped toilet. A very loud splash followed by silence. I panicked. Did the soundtrack birds stop singing?

"Where have you been, Billy? We have about two minutes. Come on." "Savi, I dropped one of the battery-packs into the jungle river . . . " "You what?" "Into the toilet." "You What? Oh, here we are." Our spot, on time, everything synchronized. I see the runners too, at least one of them, I see Aaron, the camera man—he's ready for his hand-off, eyes darting around. Mickey is coming down from the mountain. There's that pause before the Christmas Day Parade that we planned for. Hordes of Disney characters waiting in their carriages and cars somewhere behind the façade of the perfect Main Street USA, ready to go—Mickey and Minnie and Snow White and Goofy and Aladdin and Pocahontas and Pluto and Donald and Jiminy Cricket and Tinkerbell and Dumbo and Simba and Hercules and Cinderella and Winnie the

Pooh and Eeyore and the Beauty and the Beast and Peter
Pan and . . .

"There they are!" The long double line of brilliant red-
robed singers shown in the sun. And ready for the
parade—the thousands of kids up on shoulders,
munchkins with solid gold Mickey-ear hats for the
anniversary, mothers making seating arrangements on
curbs, fathers looking into the distance, strollers and
wheelchairs and 1880s surreys with the fringe on top
getting out of the way . . . opening up the street for the big
moment . . . and here come our friends, humming a
fiendish Silent Night. The Christmas cheer goes up from
the two sides of the street. James and Savitri trade a signal
and the Stop Shopping Gospel Choir swings into
"Shopocalypse! Shopocalypse! WHOA! WHOA! WHOA!"

I was deep in my reverie of gratitude. I'm so proud of
all of us—my friends—for braving the dark doings of this
place. Everyone was cheering to the Shopocalypse Song.
"Do you feel the heat in this shopping list?/The neighbors
fade into the shopping mall./The oceans rise but I, I must
buy it all./Shopocalypse. Shopocalypse . . . "

I walked to the front of the choir. The gleeful intensity
of it all felt really good. I was scared, but the choir was
already something beyond scared, this was High Church.
The angels were singing in the heavens as we danced into

the center of this world-straddling corporation. We turned and the thousands embraced—cheered for—the choir, apparently thinking that we were from some local church. I started to preach: "Isn't this wonderful. We asked Santa—and Santa gave us what we wanted. And now here we are in Disneyland! Look at this Main Street. Main Street USA! Here we are in the midst of this prosperity! But wait a minute, something's wrong! Back in America, it's not this prosperous. The main streets are shuttered, empty, outsourced!"

People were listening. You could see their faces light up when they caught our Stop Shopping message. Parents were speaking to each other over the top of their kids' heads, discussing if this was OK. Some people bent over laughing, clapping, thumbs-upping. Others angry. "How can you do this on Christmas Day! You should be . . ." Yes, yes. "Stop Shopping! Let's slow down our consumption, children."

A person in uniform was already by my side. This was a lady with a long braid, a person who may have been a hippie once in her Life. She was Disney security. So can she really arrest me? I don't remember what she said. I could see the runners working their way through the crowd with their cassettes. We're into the second song, "What Would Jesus Buy?/Buy the Heaven, Get the

Hell/What's in the window? What's for sale?/Back away from the product/The shoppers start to wail, wail, wail/Find a way to give/Do we shop till we die? Another kind of gift . . ."

The choir is floating like angels, serious like bandits. I kept preaching, trying to sum up the lessons of our month-long, country-long Shopocalypse Tour, because I knew I had seconds to go.

Here's the good news!
We forgot something, but now we remember!
We made Christmas!
Santa is our creation!
We made Mickey Mouse!
We built cars, wars . . . . And what we made,
We can unmake. We can change!
For so many years, change came from
Technology, and investment, and advertising campaigns!
We made all that too! The good news?
It's not too late to take back the responsibility of changing
Our lives! Let's take back change!
Isn't that the best gift we can give each other this
Christmas? Yes, let's give each other Change!
Merry Christmas!

More security is now surrounding me. The police seem to be trying to form moving circles around us. I get more exuberance from the singers. We're turning around the giant Christmas tree at the end of the street and start back, now facing the Magic Castle, and I'm inside a circle of uniforms now but it only helps the drama. I'm taller, I'm still making eye contact with the crowd—I'm the raving head over the top of the police escort. Trying to go for that last tough yard: "Children, where is that product from? What about the products on the shelves in Disneyland? Go and find the label! This is Main Street USA! Where is it made? Sri Lanka! China! The Philippines! We can't afford to be apolitical anymore! Where are these things from? Why is our Main Street dead? Why is the weather so hot? Why is there no work? Why do we keep buying?"

It's not long now. The circle is tightening. I'm being read the Trespassing Act, the Disorderly Conduct Act . . . the word "Private Property"—the scurrilous refuge of the powerful is repeatedly invoked. There are maybe twenty-five cops. Several of them are giving us speeches that they are REAL police, "from the jurisdiction of the City of Anaheim, California, and I do hereby instruct you, under the authority . . ." They do have a problem in that so many people here are in costumes, from police to 1880s sideshow barkers and piano-pounding dandies, and all the way up the fabulist ladder to the dancing hippos in Fantasia—all in the pay of the Mouse.

I don't remember much from the final blur, except the pain in my arm from the twisting and handcuffing. The choir started singing the First Amendment song. Savitri was trying to keep the choir out of the arrest area because we have several vulnerable green card and student visa people. Some of our camera people came in close to get the arrest, and others held back, lining up with the tourists and their cameras.

I found myself sitting on a stool behind the fabled Disney surface, back in Realityland, the paved stinking back area. The people aren't required to smile back here, and seem relieved not to. I was looking directly into the face of a bored and bitter Snow White, throwing down a cigarette butt and crushing it into the pavement with her glowing white shoe. More of the paraders were waiting there, with their carriages and horses, off schedule now—because of us.

We are staring at each other, the forty or fifty Disney characters and I. There was a bit of the "Dr. Livingston, I presume" in this moment. I'm slumped on the stool, breathing hard, heart beating heavily in my full preacher suit. The bad Elvis hair has now collapsed down over my ears. The cop to my right is calling me names. But the actors in the costumes, lined up for the Christmas Day parade, are softly regarding me and wondering. As my breathing comes back to normal, I return the open interest. I'm thinking to myself . . . I wouldn't be so terribly out of place if I jumped in there, between Jiminy Cricket and Goofy. After all, Billy Sunday evangelists were very much a part of the 1880s Main Street, but then Disney would have to make a morally neutral one. We start smiling at each other a little. Tinkerbell waves her wand a bit, and I nod, with my arms behind my back. Suddenly I want to say I love them so much. I care for them so much. I'm swooning with the feeling that, just, *how do we all do this?* There's a way of looking at the people in our country that we're all actors chasing our great Oscar-winning scene, all of us, even in an hour-long traffic jam, even in a lonely wandering off after a romance ends, even while calling our mothers on the phone. Trying to get into the park. Trying to get up to the top of the mountain in fifty years.

Bing Crosby finally puts down the microphone. White Christmas has stopped. I shout, "I'd prefer a darker shade of pale!" The Anaheim jailer says I'm getting out tonight. Oh, I'm glad. There's always more shopping to stop.

THE WINTER SERVICE

A Tribute to Buy Nothing Day,

OR

Stop Shopping, Start Giving

—◆◆—

"The best things in life aren't things."

—JUDITH LEVINE, *NOT BUYING IT*

A VERILY, VERILY POINT FOR THE FAITHFUL AT DINO'S,
THE LAST NEIGHBORHOOD BLUES JOINT IN VEGAS.
ON THE RIGHT, TRUMPETER MARK TIPTON, IN HIS
CLINT-WITH-SNEAKERS LOOK.

LET US PRAY.
Give us the bravery to dismantle Santa, Mickey, and the daily retail grosses. May the gift at Christmas not be the end of Life. Lend us the insight to see how cockeyed and backwards things have gotten. The resources are here—we are the upright, big-brained animal. God gave us the smarts. How did giving become taking? How did the celebration of Life become murder?

Amen.

And now, the congregation will rise. Let's read together The Beatitudes of Buylessness:

Blessed are the Consumers, for you shall be free from Living By Products.

Blessed are you who stumble out of branded Main Streets, for you shall find lovers not downloaded and oceans not rising.

Blessed is the ordinary citizen who holds onto a patch of public Commons, for you are the New World.

Blessed is the artist who is not corporate sponsored,

for you shall give birth to warm fronts of emotion and breakthroughs of Peace.

Blessed are you who confuse "Consumerism" with "Freedom," for you shall be delighted to discover the difference.

Blessed are the advertisers and commercial celebrities, for you are waiting for the remarkable restfulness of honesty.

Blessed are city neighborhoods that people have flown from in fear, for your children shall return to illuminate the dark economy.

Blessed are the workers in the supermalls, for the town your employers killed shall come back to Life!

Blessed is the breadwinner with outsourced dreams who sits in the SUV stuck in a Christmas from Hell, for this year a gift will set you free.

Blessed are you who are pinned under the gaze of the four supermodels of the Shopocalypse, for you shall transcend the media and dance in the streets.

Blessed are the young women in sweatshops, for the things you make will fly you like magic evening gowns to the City of Light.

Blessed are you who disturb the customers, for in doing so, you are loving them.

Amen.

Greetings, children.

Buy Nothing Day is the day after Thanksgiving. The Devil calls it Black Friday.

Thanksgiving, Buy Nothing Day, Black Friday—a traffic jam of three holidays within forty-eight hours, but all three are deep in the tsunamic white shadow of Christmas.

As the sun rises over Brooklyn, Thanksgiving is already a distant memory, or a hangover. Christmas looms above us, a month away but already here. Look at the neighborhood: hollow flirting plastic deer and balloony Caspers and little tinselly lights from China, Mickey and Minnie and St. Nick waving Old Glory and Britney in a Santa bra . . .

I am pausing a moment before the daunting force of that. Then I hear a moan. Savitri is waking up.Well, there are Stop Shopping singers and activists and writers all over New York City waking up right now, readying themselves for the contested space between the innocence of dreaming and the commercial sparklers up here in America . . .

It is the fourth quarter in the corporate world, when the retail income gushes after Thanksgiving and sends the businesses into the Black—at dawn today they are already announcing the early shopping returns. Mall manager Pat M. steps up to the cameras on my television, "We got here at four a.m. and opened up at five." Gentle Pat seems to truly believe that he is at the beating heart of our national culture, that this morning after Thanksgiving is our defining moment. He says, "They line up hundreds deep, long before dawn, still bloated in the stomach from a mother-lode helping of turkey, stuffing, mashed potatoes, yams, corn, peas, and cranberry sauce." The TV blonde Cheryl V. spits on the microphone like she is witness to the Bunker Hill of the American Dream. She reports that shoppers are trampling each other, "we have fist fights in Florida and windows breaking in Ohio." The mall manager says he regrets the violence, but by gosh you have to admire the ferocity of that All-American running and grabbing—for Amazing Amanda, for the new X-Box 360, and various robotic puppies.

And so Consumerism's month begins. It happened last year, too, and the year before that. But this time, there is a quality to this media coverage that everyone involved is holding on for dear Life. Oh, we are ready to trudge back into the candy canes, but this Christmas some point seems to be absurdly tipping. It is as if an unknown product has crept into the store and taken its place on the dazzling Christmas shelves. Maybe this will be the year that media culture and the arts and fashion and—all these shapes and sounds we follow—all become just TOO MUCH. Maybe hours of traffic jams and miles of suburban sameness will leave millions of us unable to summon our annual enthusiasm. "Oh, not again . . ."

Savitri is up and we put on Coltrane, "My Favorite

Things." We get dressed and go. We walk up the footbridge over the expressway and make our way to the F Train. Today is our ultimate workday. What am I saying? This month is our ultimate work *month*. We're packed and, last we heard, the buses are nearly here. We won't be back in our neighborhood until the end of the year.

Our friends up and down these streets will do the holidays right. This is a zip code of civil servants, lots of pensioners, teachers and cops, and the streets are full of kids. There is no *scene* here, not much gentrification yet, and thank god. Some might call this the interior suburbs. However, we don't only go to "the city" to find the arts or some traditional sophistication. This is Brooklyn. Let them come here. Right here we have Prospect Park, the more beautiful Olmstead Park, and Savitri and I live between the park lake and the vast rest in Green Wood Cemetery. If we ever lack for originals in our immediate neighborhood, well, we're about a block from where Lenny Bernstein's body is still singing "There's a Place for Us!" and Lola Montes is dancing her Spider Dance and Monty Clift is studying the mustangs in *The Misfits*.

Savitri says, "Here it is." We can feel the faint sound, a pushy underground wind. So the train screeches to a halt in the old station and we get in and sit there. As we slide under Brooklyn, under the hill where the first big battle of the American Revolution was fought, Savitri and I look at each other and we know. Here in a subway car, we are not just traveling west toward Manhattan, but we're slouching toward Disneyland. We'll try to do something that we've talked about since we began this ten years ago: How to confront the consumer somewhere between the SUV and the cash register? How to force out singing and preaching across the parking lots of the United States into the lobbies, into the chains and Big Boxes?

And now, from the Holy Writ, our reading for today's message, as preached that morning on the F Train to my not-so-startled neighbors.

> Buy Nothing today. Buy Nothing on Black Friday. Today is Buy Nothing Day, let's slow down our consumption. Buy Nothing. Back away from the product, turn away, walk, walk, to freedom. Children, remember, this shopping season . . . You don't have to buy something to give something! What is a gift really? And if you need to spend that money, well do it in an independent store, in the neighborhood, not in some Big Box or chain store . . . Amen?

The F is our home train. The folks here know they happen to live on the same train as that preacher who looks like a country singer. They are patient with me. And they figure I'm going to Times Square to preach there on the sidewalk. And, actually, they are right.

We're waiting to surface by the flagship stores on Fifth Avenue in Manhattan. Let us join the sinning crowd pushing through the concrete, steel, and glass canyons aroused by a Black Friday purchase. Here comes our stop.

Savitri and I walk through thousands of people, many of whom are, in essence, meditating on a purchase, reaching the exquisitely gloved hand out to fondle the product. Shopping is the American yoga, an alchemy of bovine drifting and predatory alertness. I am beginning to growl, "Slow down your consumption, Children . . . watch it . . . be careful now . . . slow it down . . . " Savitri says, "Not now! Not yet!"

This is my second Buy Nothing parade here in Glitzville in three years. Of course, Fifth Avenue has a new presentation each and every shopping season. But even "New and Improved" doesn't sell anything anymore. The aesthetic is more on the scale of "Ye who dare enter here, ye never had a Life before."

Here is the Plaza, and quite a good number of people who want to Buy Nothing—in this, the Fifth Year of Our Terror, in the Fourth Quarter of the Shopocalypse—are here.

The Stop Shopping Gospel Choir is here, singing What Would Jesus Buy? Red-robed, and with a fine holy fury, they rock back and forth on the steps of the fountain, already climbing up into their radical harmonies, with their hands up high and breath steaming from their upturned faces. The comedy of it, and the sneaky seriousness, too, has a smiling crowd studying them in concentric rings: people, press, and police. As Savitri and I wade into the Breughel festival of it all, we have to honor how remarkable it is that these centuries of bronze behorsed soldiers and gold-winged goddesses and grand Central Park oaks and even more than that—all the torpid reverence that the tourist industry has caked upon 59th and Fifth—how all this could be so transformed.

And now we push toward the Stonehenge of Logos, Times Square, the Devil's Lair. And leaving from here, going west like every good red-blooded American, first going west from Fifth Avenue to the Great White Way, but soon we'll be going west from the Apple into a month of supermall nation . . . all the way to Christmas in Disneyland. Help us. Be with us, God Who Is Not A Product, as we lower ourselves down into ultimate Shopasm. We are going to a paved continent of endless identical details, the architecture of a great nation gone bonkers. CO_2 exhaust and tinsel, Mickey Mouse and cross-addicted hangovers, all on the credit card of plastic, all paid for with lost lives, drifting souls, and that all-embracing BUYING.

May we, somehow, Stop Shopping.

Amen and Strange-a-lujah!

Here on Fifth Avenue, our Christmas parades collide. The Buy Nothings are set to march directly into the browsing Buy

Everythings. We get the high sign from Savitri and begin to high-step down the glowing canyon of consumption, Fifth Avenue, while Shopocalypse! Shopocalypse! rings in the air. We're walking into the Christmas shopping season, singing this pulsing song. It will be our anthem for The Shopocalypse Tour.

Right now, we are a crowd of a few hundred, stretching back half of the block, with the press jostling at the edges and the police riding their scooters single-file in the street. I'm trying to key on what I see, responding to one shopper at a time, keeping a foreground conversation going—"Let's be conscious with the spending, alright?"—and raring back and filling the street with sound. We pass the General Motors building with FAO Schwartz next to it, and the Coca-Cola building with its high-end Italian and French shops and on to the Nike and Gap anchor stores, which are rolled out like big art galleries. Now the choir starts a rhythmic song-chant, "Stop Shopping Start Living!" These sexy, crazy people, singing and singing and singing, rev up the reverend.

We have almost the full choral group, about thirty singers. Since Buy Nothing Day is a Friday, some folks can't get here from their day-jobs. A number of the faithful work in midtown, or near a train, so they can donate a lunch hour to the Buy Nothing festivities. But this is a good New York group: singers from all five boroughs, singers from Uganda,

South Korea, Sweden, Venezuela, Serbia, Puerto Rico, and Ireland. You might say they are showing international (let's say universal) concern about American shopping. The drums are rolling, and the trumpet is on the throne. I never can help myself: I try to check out the response of the shoppers, screwing up their faces to hear us. "Will we drive fast all night, to the wilderness, to the wilderness? Will we die of fright when the logos hiss?" The logos hiss? Honey, have you ever heard a logo hiss? Hmmm . . . . In the middle distance, we sense the tourists edging forward from Donald Trump's lobby, reaching for disposable cameras, oh, these must be New York characters . . .

Journalists hurry alongside us, cruising in and out of our parade with their sleek, black techno-boxes. A singer in a hammy mood, of which we have many in the choir to choose from—say, Jerry Goralnick from the Living Theater or Gina Figueroa from the Loisida or Urania Mylonas from the Hungry March Band—is usually ready with liberating sound bites. But you have to march with us, keep up! And you can't shop while you talk with us! Notice that? So we try to imagine humanity in the shiny lenses and microphones of CNN and the *Times* and the French and the Germans and BBC and FOX 5—Eye Witness News—we try to preach to a distant congregation out in the world, to the family trapped in a glass and metal bubble for hours with nothing but a dashboard radio telling them to BUY, or maybe we can reach a citizen alone in a house with the TV on, with shopping offering its illusion to salve the loneliness.

> *Put your hand on the television screen, I feel there's a sister in Kansas and you want to GRAB YOUR PLASTIC AND RUN OUT THE DOOR! You come and pray with the Reverend, walk with me through the gates to the UTOPIA OF ABSTINENCE FROM CLUTTER! It might be confusing at first . . . here, don't you worry, we'll do this difficult thing together . . .*

The managers and retail cops—compassion here, they get paid *zilch*—come out from behind the neurotic elves and haughty half-naked mannequins in the Christmas show windows. As if our flaming choir passing into their window space is any weirder than what they offer up for public review? Oh, but they paid for the airspace, I see. A Starbucks official steps in front of us. "You can't record Starbucks imagery in your cameras! That's private property! We'll have to ask for your tape!" At which point he is engulfed in the Hot Red Angels of Buylessness. So there's nothing he can do. He is left to worry about the sensitive tape whirring within our cameras. He steps back into his doorway, back under the scaly skirts of the famous Starbucks logo, the nippleless mermaid, the private property with air-brushed privates.

I'm trying to not be annoyed that the press wants me to preach on demand. Just anything Rev, go ahead. Oh, I'm sorry but will you do it again? Can you slow down a moment? You don't mind if I wire you .... Reverend just shout Change-a-lujah one more time so we can set our levels! We are televised every which way, but its not quite the same televangelism as Jimmy Swaggart here. And of course the police have THEIR cameras, no logos on their Darth Vader deep gray.

The police can ask their large silent friends the skyscrapers to get the master shots. The buildings of New York City are now bristling with surveillance cameras cocked down like they know something about us pedestrians. You can see them up there on the ledges, sharing a malevolent gleam in the eye with the gargoyles who slouch next to them. We citizens are cast as villains in movies that will go straight to video. They say that each of us creates the equivalent of fourteen feature films while walking through the course of an ordinary day in Manhattan. The buildings are soaking up our images, the patterns of our wanderings, who we kiss and why and who we shout at and who we pay. This huge film project, turning the skyline itself into a peeping Tom. It's for security, we're told, but we know that ultimately the Patriot Act has it's evil twin information sucker: corporate marketing. Someday it will all be fed into Christmas.

But wait a minute—ARE WE COMPLAINING OR ARE WE CHANGING? One idea: let's give them a show. There's a way we can walk down here that will change the picture up there. What is our update of the Boston Tea Party, the march from Selma to Montgomery, or Gandhi's long hike to the sea?

It's hard to take back Christmas. It's not easy to compete with these comely mannequins either. We try. One of our group has a blinding Cat-In-The-Hat costume, another has cantilevered her hair to alarming proportions, and she's got on the Full Chicken herself, a doppelbilly, as we say. We all move forward, clapping and singing across the million-dollar-a-foot Fifth Avenue real estate, visually and sonically prying into the traditional ritual of this famous street. "Buy Nothing!" We are saying the thing that would obstruct this key American fundamentalism, the retailing-into-the-Black of Christmas. Saying the words that would undo it all—Buy Nothing!—as if those words really had power. But then, just having that transgressive thought and expressing it—Buy Nothing!—this does seem to have a powerful fascination to worshippers in the Church of Fifth Avenue, the cathedral of consumption. Isn't shopping the thing we're not supposed to question at all? People are stopped across the street, leaning out of windows. "What are they saying? Buy Nothing. Oh. Buy Nothing? That's what they are saying? Really? But that's incredible . . . . Imagine . . . buying . . . Nothing . . ."

Now we are trapping a gilt crowd—forty million dollars worth of credit—in the front alcove of the Trump Towers. Superconsumers waiting for the parade to pass, sinners who catch the preacher's eye. "You are MY church, children! Before we come to today's message. Let me ask you a question. IS THERE ANYONE HERE AMONG US WHO HAS NOT BEEN CHASED DOWN AND KILLED BY A DISCOUNTED LUXURY ITEM? Welcome to Buy Nothing Day. Twenty-four hours of absolution, we stand inside America but not its hypnotizing paranoid GULPING-EVERYTHING economy. I'M NOT BUYING IT. Can I hear some of you New Yorkers say "I'M MAD AS HELL AND I'M NOT BUYING IT ANYMORE?" Amen . . . Well, got some nervous laughter, anyway.

We stop at crosswalks, wait for the glowing red hand to become a little white man—but sometimes the police stop traffic for us, wave us across and smile conspiratorially. "I spend too much too, Reverend! And thanks for the overtime! I can use the dough to score some stupid gifts! Reverend! Forgive me!" You are forgiven, my children. We are all sinners. But I've got a question, guys and gals of the badge. How come I'm not in jail yet? You usually have me in cuffs by now. I was arrested the last two Buy Nothing Days, in 2003 and 2004, but this year, it seems, possibly not! What's going on? Savitri is running to the front of the procession and then back, trying to keep the shape and flow. I tend to get too far out ahead because the preaching energizes my legs, and then suddenly I'm alone and it's easy for the police to surround me, which is how I got detained by ten seven-foot-tall German infantrymen in Berlin last year. Savitri pushes me back into the scarlet army of harmonizing gospelettes.

Then a hand reaches out and takes my bullhorn, "You've got no permit for that." I have my usual response. "Yes, here's my permit. In fact I have it memorized. Do you have your notebook ready? It will be on the test. Here it goes: 'Congress shall make no law respecting an establishment of religion, or prohibiting the free exercise thereof, or abridging the freedom of speech, or the press, or THE RIGHT OF THE PEOPLE PEACEABLY TO ASSEMBLE, and to petition the govern-ment for redress of grievances.' Is this familiar? Do you feel a haunting familiarity in those words?" By now Savitri has pushed us by and waylaid the police with her special boys-in-blue Tai Chi. I have to turn to my other bullhorn, the one I carry in my lungs. Meanwhile, doppelbilly Monica has begun a sermon about child slavery in West Africa in front of a high-end chocolate shop. The choir has sunk to its knees, and in an instant, church and a crowd has gathered. Slavery? Children? Chocolate? And then I see the steaming tar.

Along Fifth Avenue, at 55th, they are laying down and rolling into smoothness a new layer of macadam, and it needs an Exorcism. The choir and I lay on our hands, over the edges of this East Coast La Brea lake, while the road repair guys are shoveling the clods of black along the edges of the curbs and into the pot-holes. "Oil covers everything. We breathe it. It smooths the way for us, or so we believe. Let's start our Oil Exorcism by promising each other that we won't kill for it any-more. Gentlemen, with your shovels and big heavy rollers and oil-caked jumpsuits, we know you've got a job to do and a family. But pray with us now. Will you? Whoever gave us this gift of this oil and gas, the energy of it, the convenience of it. We are consuming it. Maybe we can consume a little less of it. But help us to stop killing for it . . ."

Just then, in midprayer, the accumulation of Fellini-esqueness from our afternoon march makes me look up at the sky for relief. A white and silver helicopter crosses the highway of blue up there between the blinding buildings. Are you an executive arriving from Greenwich, aiming at the center of his rooftop bull's-eye? Is it possible? Did you glimpse our red stain on the street, our church procession, down here deep in your shadow?

We're turning West now, towards Times Square. Loom-ing over us is the sign of the beast, 666 Fifth Avenue, home of Orrick and Carrington and an army of fierce warrior lawyers and hedge fund mathematicians who steer jet streams of money, the command post of currency exchange experts who shoot value through seventy countries in under an hour, the computers searching through local laws and rates of exchange, a white water river of money that is imbued with its own intelligence and flows and flows through the world, following the path of least resistance, returning the most profit to the unseen master up there in the air, seated at a desk behind the glass that reflects back only clouds and sky. Mammon God, your pockets are as deep as Black Friday.

We can't judge you, because we're sinners ourselves. But can we stop you? Can we stop ourselves? Can we stop shopping?

We enter Times Square, an open-air rotunda of whirling crosses and swooshes and swaying hips and animal-faces and in the middle of the struggle by corporate marketer-artists to capture . . . what? The perfect image—before which the consumer is simply helpless—stands the jaunty statue of George M. Cohan:

> I'm a Yankee Doodle Dandy.
> A Yankee Doodle, do or die.
> A real live nephew of my Uncle Sam,
> Born on the Fourth of July!

Getting down here from the fifties was itself a musical comedy. We were trying to stay on the sunny side of the street, so we're crossing and recrossing the pavement, finding that shaft of light. And all the police scooters crossed too, our shadow parade. Savitri and I keep telling them: We're not trying to escape, we just want the sun for the singers! Now, the cops are uniformed big men on little scooters who seem to move together like over-serious penguins in a synchronized swimming routine. You'll admit—funny! As we set up our final song and sermon here on the island in the storm, the police remain good-humored. They are willing to share their privatized Broadway with the permitless church clowns. Is it because on this Buy Nothing Day, unlike last year, we're not going into stores and EXORCIZING THE CASH REGISTERS? Not that I'm not tempted—I am. I'm very tempted. I've developed an erotic relationship with the cash registers of multinational corporations that is now, frankly, out of control, like good holy sex should be . . .

We are on the island between Broadway and Seventh Avenue at the end of our parade, a momentary Fabulous Worship. Brother William on guitar and Brother Derrick on vocals are performing "The Back Away Song." Like the parade's start at the Plaza, we have our peeps: the performers, the people, the press, and the police. But here in Times Square we don't have a Greek god on a pedestal. We have a bottle of Coca-Cola that rises higher than the Statue of Liberty and has smoke pouring from its mouth. We have a thousand such gigantic images buffed up for the final siege of Christmas. And as tiny as we are, we are still right here. Now it may not seem like it, but this is our advantage, that we are, all of us, the same size. The corporation is claiming to be a person, too, but we can do some things the corporation can't, like say hello softly and be believed. We can decide to trust each other and walk awhile together. And we can sing for you!

Nobody knows why The Great White Way still has this power. Everybody uses it because they know its here—it's like drilling oil out of the air. Oh, there's talk of a hidden Indian river under Broadway. Cultural historians discuss Tin Pan Alley or the thousands of songs and story plots that rose up from these footlights. I've studied the hand-written Record of Conveyances back to the first purchases of land. The John L. Norton farm, originally under what became Broadway block 1010–1019, after constructions and fires and mortgages and refinancings, finally flowered into Goofys and Sleepys and Donald Ducks and the thousand screaming anthropomorphized animals now dancing on the shelves of Disney's 42nd Street address. Sometime between the Norton farm and the Lion King—after the land was gone and the buildings were standing side by side, by about the time of the Civil War, judging from the building permits that were requested of the city, the floor plans, the mysterious Winthrop law firm that lurks through generations—it looks as if the Disney store was a whore house.

"Get ready for the sermon. Are you *ready*?" Oh yes, almost.

Although the stages and the streets are privatized, although every one of us has turned into a tourist, half-dazed by staring, accompanied by a cop on a cell phone with hand-cuffs on his belt, the power remains here, in the Great White Way. Come here and scream your Truth. The Puritans of Consumption haven't been able to stop actual people, arriving every hour, under their own power. Here we are, in our bodies. And every god, every fake Rolex, every charcoal portrait artist and break-dancer with an inverted hat for cash—and every last kind of sex—is still traded in shadows that open up within shouting distance of the four-story Diane Sawyer and MTV logos and a grinning Richard Branson from Virgin. They were all told that Broadway would be their private orchestra pit.

Unsanctioned talk—the most dangerous god of all—is happening here. . . . That's where the power is in this amazing place that is not privatized, is not yet purchased. There's the hope.

We feel, in this moment, like the last American crowds, pushed around and pushed again and now washed up on this glowing corporate shore. They tell us to keep our brains and our pockets empty, and leave the real talking and listening, the real singing and preaching to these giant products/ celebrities/logos that reverberate their signals back and forth across Broadway. That's their Orwellian model, the logos talking to each other up in the air, with people below pre-persuaded, just consuming, and not in the loop of power. Logo to logo, transacting: the perfect economy.

Times Square is becoming Christmas. Angels are appearing in the Diamondvision walls. Lambs and Santas are pulled around the elastic horizons up there—an altar upon which our way of seeing the world is ritualized into acceptance. We come in a great crowd and we learn to see this way, together. Then as individuals and as families, we go into what is left of our private lives having accepted an absurd perspective. We are Consumerized. We have bought everything. And now we are locked in a focus that can confuse a war with a video game. We make decisions to kill our own towns, and leave our children surrounded by parking lots and on-ramps and their master logos . . .

"Alright, let's preach now," Savitri says.

I start touching the hands of the smiling strangers slowly, in that pastoral way, staying with the eyes, always slowing down, welcoming our parishioners, "I'm glad to see you made it to church this week," "Good to see you this week, I've become concerned about your shopping sins . . ."

Yes, we have been fooled for a while, but we know we are very close to change. Moments away. Words away. We're just a bit out of practice and we have to help one another recognize what we can do.

"The buses are ready . . ." Savitri says.

WILL WE SURVIVE THE
SHOPOCALYPSE?

WHAT A PRIVILEGE, WHEN FACING THE SHOPOCALYPSE,
TO HAVE A JOYOUS GOSPEL CHOIR TO FALL BACK ON.

AND SO THE REVOLUTION of Exalted Embarrassment has begun. The silence of the products, the deep put-on of the products, is no longer the monarch before which we grab and swipe and save and spend. In fact, we are belly laughing profoundly. We are watching the amazed wandering away of our hands. Our consumerized gestures have had some kind of century storm blown through them. We're just NOT BUYING. And why aren't we buying? Because YOU, CHILDREN, YOU STOPPED ME. And I am from the Church of the Necessary Interruption and I am returning the favor. I break you from your mindless fondling of the bottle of something or other that you thought you would buy. You look up, giggling, perhaps nauseous, then you pull away from the product. Can we even remember what that product was? It was powerful and silent, and introduced to us by happy famous faces along the walls of the streets.

Can I tell you what that product was doing to us? It protruded itself into our hands, sexual contact from a science fiction world that is ruled by only one bewildering value:

per-share return to distant investors. But for you and me, that
DO-I-BUY-IT? MOMENT is the last chance for change, the
stress fracture in the commodity wall, the nearly invisible
actual voting booth of America—and the only glimpse we'll
get of revolution when revolution is not yet content for a
product called Revolution. Amen?

And we Back Away. Carefully we edge away from the
predator's glossy eye, from the commercial hologram, from
the great organization chart of averaged desire. Yes, this is
the day our shopping stopped in Aisle F. Back near the
mousse gels. Back in the instant soup. Back in the uranium-
depleted bullets. We don't say, "Today is a good day to die."
We say, "Today is a good day NOT TO BUY!" Oh, it is Buy
Nothing Day in America! And the Rumsfelds of retail don't
know how to scramble their jets as the postconsumption
children walk slowly off the pavement. And we're not just
discussing a boycott here, we're talking about all the rest of
our lives, the sensuous continuum beyond shopping. Not
buying is the Practice, now where, oh where, is the Temple?

As the artist known as Jesus once said, "Our body is
God's Temple, which he hath created." As the poet Robert
Creeley once said, "The Plan is the Body. The Plan is the
Body." As Emma Goldman once said, "Love is the Law." As
Jimmy Swaggart once said on his knees with his aghast wife
staring at him in the front pew, "Oh! God Almighty! Oh!

Please! Dear! I'm so sorry, Dear!" And as the advertisers said when the doughboys returned from The Great War, "You need to deodorize your armpits or you won't ascend to THE LAND OF LARGE WHITE APPLIANCES."

Back Away from the Shopocalypse and you are not merely spared. You've got your body back. That's where the fun starts, my children. That's the SPRING BREAK where banned books fly again in great flocks, the libraries solemnly removing the fig leaves and refusing the Homeland spies a computer readout of our curiosity. This is the Love of Life that is a couple miles beyond the strategic atmospheres in Big Boxes and the counter help terrified into dullness. We become, what?—Unbuying! Damn! We BUY NOTHING.

We hope that we will still have the privilege to not buy before we are blown off the oil rig, drowning in a petro-chemical lake, PUSHED OFF THE PRODUCT, our lesson from the wind, the waves, and the fire. Consumerism's convenience must wreak its violence, its Death by gas and oil. The Shopocalypse, right on schedule.

If we keep shopping, then Katrina and Rita will become just two more products on the shelf, a steal for $300 billion. The marketers are astonished that we're still buying, even as the waters rise. Oh, we struggle to awake from our Consensual Hypnosis . . . our Consumer Narcosis . . .

We have become one great shopper with one hell of a

shopping problem. We have everything we need, but we do a U-turn and drive back to the big box to buy the Earth. And there it is! On the shelf! We roll it out across the parking lot, but then we just can't get it into the car.

Right at this moment, that's where we are. The Earth won't fit in the back of our 4 x 4. We're pushing and pushing. Yes, we sense that something is wrong. It's not like the signal is unclear. We have time—Seconds? Years? Centuries? The pavement extends as far as we can see. It waits for us to come home with our purchase. But we stopped our shopping. We stand there. We are feeling a glorious sensation.

CHANGE-A-LUJAH!

AT THE END OF OUR SERVICES, SISTER VALERIE SINGS
THE *THANK YOU SONG*, AND WE ARE GRATEFUL THAT YOU'VE
READ OUR BOOK ... AMEN AND PRAISE BE!

GLOSSARY

ADVERTOPIA—The Promised Land in an Ad.

ART ATTACK—Any kind of performance that carries anti-consumerist information into property controlled by real estate speculators, multinational corporations, or the government. *The art attack on the Starbucks in the Trump Tower lobby brought out goons in polyester plaid suits.*

BACKING AWAY FROM THE PRODUCT—The religious practice of the Stop Shopping Church, in which a believer reaches out for, holds, then retreats and flees from, a product, ad, or celebrity. *I backed away from the product, and Holy Oddness waited for me on the other side.*

BEATITUDES OF BUYLESSNESS—The song and political strategy in which all are forgiven their consumption. *And then they sang "Blessed are those who confuse Consumerism with Freedom, for they shall be delighted to discover the difference!"*

CHANGE-A-LUJAH!—A gospel shout that celebrates and causes change.

CHOSEN PEOPLE—A nation creates a God that creates a nation that creates a God that creates a nation. *Chosen People suffer a terrible weakness for believing their own advertising.*

THE CHURCH OF WHA? WHAT'S GOING ON?—A faith based on visiting the Big Bang, the personal amazement at the moment of being born. Also known as The Church of Don't Born Again Me Cuz One Time Is Enough!

EVIL—When we don't maximize the freedom of others.

EXALTED EMBARRASSMENT—The thrill of the personal breakthrough of the practice of Holy Oddness in a public place, indicating the scandalized feelings of the practitioner of a retail intervention or the embarrassment of the shoppers witnessing it.

FABULOUS UNKNOWN—A way of worshipping (Fabulously) this remarkable thing called Unexplained Life, while avoiding the violence of a continuous God, especially the three desert Gods with their famous anger issues.

GODSIGHTINGS—An experience that takes place in the middle of a consumer's day which is unexplained, miraculous, and not-a-product. *I was waiting for the bus, and my 714 stories starting coming up, and a stranger from across the street shouted SEVEN HUNDRED AND FOURTEEN STORIES.*

THE IMMEDIATE LIFE—The soul-saved flipside of The Mediated Life. *Spalding asked, how can we raised an unmediated child? How to stay in the Immediate Life?*

THE IMPRESARIO OF SHOCKING EVOLUTION AND HOLY HILARIOUSNESS—A phrase used by Reverend Billy to call the Fabulous Unknown into the roomful of the faithful.

LORDS OF CONSUMPTION—A Lord of the Rings type phrase that sums up the evil twin fundamentalisms of corporate marketing and apocalyptic Christianity.

ODD—Found in the phrases "Put the Odd Back in God" or "Oddly Holy" or the old Muslim saying "God loves the Odd." Odd has as many uses in the Stop Shopping tradition as Inuits have words for the snow that has vanished.

POP—The Point of Purchase, site of Reverend Billy's Exorcisms, the cash register and sales counter area generally, the scale, bagging station, the scanner, the credit card swiper and signature window and Angelina and Brad's latest baby.

PRODUCT—Anything whose meaning to others is defined by its price, image, or ability to cause violence.

PRODUCT GODS—These are the superior beings which can be endlessly manufactured, shipped, priced, and sold. The opposite of the Odd God. *APPLE was my Product God, back when I thought John and Yoko sold iBooks.*

PRODUCT HUMAN—A compassionate reference to celebrities.

PURITANS OF CONSUMPTION—Refers to the creators of the distance between desire illustrated to sell products and desire itself.

PUSH PRAYER—The request to an all-powerful God for help in a time of need is accomplished by taking control of the situation. *My push prayer was both my request and my action.*

714 STORIES—The building blocks, the DNA, of a post-product personality. The 714 stories deep inside us were self-selected from our first moments of life as our personal glories or traumas. *Marketers try to delete our 714 stories, or attach product placement deals to our oldest impressions.*

SHOPOCALYPSE—Western Civilization's recent way of life, or vast drunk party, which is a terminal process in the life systems of the earth, where the importance of fourth quarter corporate earnings control any possible resistance to mass suicide. *The Shopocalypse will try to extend its pathology with the strategical flashing of Heidi Klum's thighs.*

SUPERMALL OF ETERNAL CONVENIENCE—Where the hordes of fundamentalist consumers will go for Eternal Life On Credit during the Shopocalypse.

STRANGE-A-LUJAH—A gospel shout that often follows Change-a-lujah in the Stop Shopping choir's hymns, indicating the need to go deeper into the Odd.

THE UNKNOWN—The condition which precedes birth and follows death. It accompanies us through Life as well. This is where all UnBuying belief comes from, including biological evolution.

ACKNOWLEDGMENTS

The Shopocalypse Tour, subject of much of this book, was made possible by Todd and Jedd Wider, in their stewardship of the Frankel Foundation. We thank the helpers of our performance community: Willie Monaghan, Michael Rosen, Martha Wilson, Marion Weber, Jonathan Moll, Aaron Sosnick, Laurence Singer, and all the patient board members of our theater company.

Those who advised and coaxed and edited: Clive Priddle and David Patterson, our editors at PublicAffairs, and of course Melissa Raymond, the designers, sales folks, and other friends up there at the end of the toxic hallway on the thirteenth floor.

Thanks to Colin Robinson, who first persuaded me to attempt books, and edited the first one. William Clark, my literary agent, kept the book alive and found a taker. Thanks especially to Urania Mylonas for proofing prowess and finding love quotes in every corner of the world.

Thanks to my fabulous partner, Savitri D, and to Julie Talen, my sister, and to Shanti Durkee and Michael O'Neil for the daily care and feeding of this unlikely church. As for the choir and band to whom the book is dedicated—they are the very hippest co-conspirators in radical joy.

PublicAffairs is a publishing house founded in 1997. It is a tribute to the standards, values, and flair of three persons who have served as mentors to countless reporters, writers, editors, and book people of all kinds, including me.

I.F. STONE, proprietor of *I. F. Stone's Weekly*, combined a commitment to the First Amendment with entrepreneurial zeal and reporting skill and became one of the great independent journalists in American history. At the age of eighty, Izzy published *The Trial of Socrates*, which was a national bestseller. He wrote the book after he taught himself ancient Greek.

BENJAMIN C. BRADLEE was for nearly thirty years the charismatic editorial leader of *The Washington Post*. It was Ben who gave the *Post* the range and courage to pursue such historic issues as Watergate. He supported his reporters with a tenacity that made them fearless and it is no accident that so many became authors of influential, best-selling books.

ROBERT L. BERNSTEIN, the chief executive of Random House for more than a quarter century, guided one of the nation's premier publishing houses. Bob was personally responsible for many books of political dissent and argument that challenged tyranny around the globe. He is also the founder and longtime chair of Human Rights Watch, one of the most respected human rights organizations in the world.

For fifty years, the banner of Public Affairs Press was carried by its owner Morris B. Schnapper, who published Gandhi, Nasser, Toynbee, Truman, and about 1,500 other authors. In 1983, Schnapper was described by *The Washington Post* as "a redoubtable gadfly." His legacy will endure in the books to come.

Peter Osnos, *Founder and Editor-at-Large*